INSTITUTIONAL FINANCE AND RURAL ARTISANS

INSTITUTIONAL FINANCE AND RURAL ARTISANS

Progress, Performance and Prospects

By

SMRUTIREKHA MOHANTY

ANMOL PUBLICATIONS PVT. LTD.
NEW DELHI - 110 002 (INDIA)

ANMOL PUBLICATIONS PVT. LTD.
4374/4B, Ansari Road, Daryaganj
New Delhi - 110 002
Ph.: 23261597, 23278000
Visit us at: www.anmolpublications.com

Institutional Finance and Rural Artisans

First Published, 2004

ISBN 81-261-1746-X

PRINTED IN INDIA

Published by J.L. Kumar for Anmol Publications Pvt. Ltd., New Delhi - 110 002 and Printed at Mehra Offset Press, Delhi.

Dedicated to

My Loving Parents

Sri Bhagaban Mohanty

and

Smt. Kamala Dei

Contents

Foreword

India is a land of arts and artisans. She has earned name and fame for wonderful artistic works and materials manufactured by most committed and devoted artisans. It is a matter of great pleasure to witness that the artisan sector is not confined to a few states of the country but it encompasses almost all the states of Indian territory. From time immemorial the artisans have struggled hard to keep their enterprise alive. However, in recent years, these units have come across with several problems, particularly after the manufacture of machine products. Of several problems the artisans have mainly faced the problem of finance. On account of the decay of the patronage by the Rajas, Maharajas and Jamidars and the exploitative character of local money lenders, the artisans have felt the pinch of dearth of finance. In order to solve the problem of finance a number of institutions after nationalisation have come into existence in the country with the mission of providing regular supply of finance for the survival of the rural artisans. Smt. Smrutirekha Mohanty did a pioneering job by studying indepthly the relationship between institutional finance and rural artisans for the development of Indian economy. It is a painstaking, laborious and indepth study by the scholar at a micro level pertaining to a subnational region. The book once published will be of immense help to academicians, researchers, administrators, planners, policymakers and general readers who have keen interest to know about the artisans, their problems and prospects for the future. I personally feel the book will open plenty of opportunities to the incoming researchers committed to study the rural artisans and institutional finance. The present volume forms a part of the Doctoral Dissertation submitted to Utkal University and examined by eminent Economists like Prof. K. Lal of Allahabad University and Prof. P.K. Chubey of Indian Institute of Public Administration, New Delhi, whose recommendations helped the scholar to bring out this present volume in published form.

—Dr. Surendra Nath Mishra
Professor of Economics,
Nabakrushna Choudhury Centre for
Development Studies (I.C.S.S.R.)
Bhubaneswar-13.

Acknowledgements

In course of my research work, I have received generous help and assistance from many quarters. I take this as an opportunity to record my thanks to persons and the institutions who have helped me in persuit of my academic work.

To begin with, I express my deep sense of gratitude to Dr. Surendra Nath Misra, Professor of Economics, Nabakrushna Choudhury Centre for Development Studies, Bhubaneswar, my guide and supervisor for his valuable guidance and encouragement.

In the course of my research work I have liberally taken the assistance from many quarters and individuals. Amongst them special mention may be made of Sri H.K. Dash, State Co-operative Bank, Bhubaneswar, Sri Rajat Singh, Reserve Bank of India, Bhubaneswar, Sri Ambika Prasad Nanda, National Bank for Agricultural and Rural Development, Sri Dolgovinda Padhi, Directorate of Textiles, Sri Saroj Pattnaik, Orissa Mining Corporation, Sri Saroj Sarangi, Directorate of Industries, Government of Orissa, Sri Sarada Das, State Co-operative Bank, Sri B.B. Mishra, Puri Gramya Bank, Sri Santosh Kumar Mohanty, CAET, O.U.A.T. for their academic help and assistance. I offer my heartfelt thanks to all of them.

I express my indebtedness and deepest gratitude to my teacher, Dr. Bidyadhar Mishra, President, Centre for Development Studies, Saheed Nagar, Bhubaneswar for giving me inspiration, encouragement and valuable suggestions in course of my research work.

I offer my thanks to Sri Subrat Mohanty for assisting me in the conduct of field study.

I have nothing but to owe my deep sense of gratitude to my parents, Sri Bhagaban Mohanty and Smt. Kamala Devi for their affection, inspiration and encouragement, without which possibly I could not have completed the research work.

I also owe my debt to my husband Sri P.K. Pattnaik, Officer, Bank of India, Patna Zone, Bihar who smilingly took all the pains and difficulties on his shoulder, the drudgery of domestic work during my absence from home in connection with my research work. To my daughter 'Honey' and son 'Happy' a word of affection for patiently overseeing my work in all these years often neglecting their personal comforts. I also have a word of affection to my brother Santosh, sisters Smita and Sushree for assisting me in my research work.

I owe my gratitude to my father-in-law Sri Baidyanath Pattnaik and mother-in-law Smt. Sorojini Pattnaik for their cooperation in this regard.

—Smrutirekha Mohanty

1
Introduction

India is a developing country which is trying to come out of the morass of poverty and backwardness slowly through developmental programmes. She has all the characteristics of under-development and backwardness common to developing countries. In order to break these vicious circle of poverty and underdevelopment, a planned process of economic development has been initiated by launching five years plans in the country. Since the beginning of planning till date India has already completed Nine Five Year Plans in the country. Under the impact of planning, the overall growth of the economy has shown a significant improvement. However, the benefits of development have not trickled down significantly to help people living at the disaggregated levels. While the benefits of development have been pocketed mostly by the urban centres and the well-to-do persons, the rural areas and the rural poor have failed to procure much benefit. In the developmental process therefore, a clear-cut distinction existed between urban and rural centres of growth and the well-to-do sections and weaker sections of the community.

In the course of planned process of economic development, it is revealed that backwardness and under-development are more deep seated in the rural areas. Rural areas are more characterised by low level of per capita income, greater incidence of poverty and unemployment, higher growth rate of population, lack of infrastructure, low productivity of agriculture and poor industrialisation and etc. In the course of planning it is realised that unless rural development takes place in a significant scale, economic development of the country will not acquire adequate momentum. Rural development, thus, lies at the root of the economic development of the country. In order to promote economic development in rural areas, the government, both Central and States have launched various schemes and programmes. Later, target oriented schemes were introduced by the Government. The objective of these target oriented schemes was to promote the development of hitherto neglected persons in the rural areas by suitable and viable schemes with a view to help them to cross the poverty line.

In the rural areas weaker sections mostly comprise of small and marginal farmers, agricultural labours, rural artisans, small businessmen and retail traders and professionally self-employed person etc. They are the designated group of weaker sections who are unable to have an annual income of Rs. 6,400. These sections of population mostly live below the officially accepted norm of poverty line.

Among the weaker sections, the rural artisans are a vulnerable group. In the past, these rural artisans had a glorious tradition. The products were mostly made out of locally available resources. The artisans had the necessary artistic qualities and expertise received from their ancestors. The products were of high aesthetic quality and those catered to the needs of a selected class of persons in the society. However, the rural artisans also produced certain items which were of common use. Some products were marketed even in overseas markets on a large scale. And most of them required comparatively less unit cost for their instalment. They are also very much labour intensive in nature. Rural artisan based units are found useful due to their high employment potential.

Hence, attention is paid, under different plan periods to develop these units. However, rural artisans engaged in these units come across with certain difficulties. Among the problems faced by rural artisans, finance is one of the chief bottlenecks that they come across. The rural artisans do not have adequate resources of their own to operate their units. Consequently they depend upon external sources of finance. Fortunately, the country has a wide spectrum of institutional financing agencies such as; Co-operative Banks, Commercial Banks and Regional Rural Banks. With active financial assistance supplied by these institutional credit agencies, there has taken place sizeable increase in the number of rural artisan units. Furthermore, production, capital investment and employment in these units too, exhibited a rising trend. However, it is observed that the performance of rural artisan units are not evenly spread throughout the country. While the progress is more concentrated in a few states, other states failed to reap the advantages. It is against this background that an humble attempt is made to analyse the role of institutional financing agencies for the development and promotion of rural artisans.

Importance of the Study

The state of Orissa, in spite of its abundant natural resources, remains economically one of the most backward states of the country. The per capita income of Orissa is much less than that of the national average. At current prices, the per capita income of Orissa was Rs. 5,625 as against Rs. 10,067 at the all India level in the year 1999-2000 at 1993-94 prices. In terms of per capita income, the place of Orissa was a little above the average obtained in the State of Bihar (Rs. 4,475 in 1999-2000). However, in comparison with other states of the country, the per capita income of Orissa was much lower.

Besides, there is also higher incidence of poverty in the state. It is noticed that about 48.6 per cent of the population in Orissa are lying below the poverty line. This is much higher than the all India average of 36.0 per cent of the population lying below the poverty line in the year 1993-94. It is further seen that poverty is more concentrated in the rural areas where 49.7 per cent of the total population live below the poverty line as against the all India average of 37.3 per cent.

Again on the basis of the per capita calorie norms recommended by the Nutrition Expert Group, which were 2435 and 2095 calories for both rural and urban areas respectively it can be said that nearly 88 per cent of the total population in the state lived below the poverty line on the eve of the Sixth Five-Year Plan. Of this nearly 65 per cent of the population are concentrated in the rural areas of the state. It is a fact that in no other states of the Indian Union incidence of poverty is so deep seated as that of in Orissa.

The total population of the state is 317 lakh as per 1991 Census. Percentagewise, Orissa accounted for 3.9 per cent of the total population of the State. According to 1991 Census it was further revealed that 38.4 per cent or a sizeable number of the state's population belonged to Scheduled Castes and Scheduled Tribes. As against this, the proportion of Scheduled Castes and Scheduled Tribes population to the total population at the all India level was 23.6 per cent. It is further revealing to note that nearly 88 per cent of the states population lived in the rural areas. This shows that urbanisation has not taken place largely in the state. It is further revealing to note that villages having less than 500 population account for 66.4 per cent of the total number of villages in the state. In these small villages alone 28.1 per cent of the total population of the state lives. The villages are not only small in size but they inhabitate a larger percentage or share of the population in the state.

Agriculture is the mainstay of the majority of population in the state. Nearly 77 per cent of the population in the state are depending upon agriculture for their livelihood and occupation. Likewise, percentage share of agricultural income in the total state income was around 59.7 per cent of the total in the year 1987-88 as per 1970-71 prices. This was 43.5 per cent in the year 1999-2000 as per 1993-94 prices. However, compared to the performance of agricultural sector at the all India level, agricultural performance at the state level is not encouraging. It is revealed that net value added in agriculture whereas stood at Rs. 2,887.2 in 1987-88 at current prices in Orissa, the same was Rs. 21,013.0 at the all India level. Similarly, per hectare average value added whereas stood at Rs. 3,326 for the period from 1985-86 to 1987-88, the same was Rs. 4,209 at the all India level. The causes of low productivity of agriculture are: inadequate irrigation facilities, low consumption of fertiliser, inadequate mechanisation etc.

Consequently more emphasis is required to be placed upon the development of industries in the rural areas. Development of industries will certainly provide the necessary stimulus for the development of rural areas including agricultural sector. Besides, agricultural development to a great extent supplements the growth of industries by supplying raw materials, food stuffs and surplus manpower. Both agriculture and industry are thus complementary to each other. Balanced development of these two sectors is a sine-qua non of economic development. Since the beginning of plan era, though more emphasis has been put on the development of large and medium scale industries, yet the emphasis on small scale, village and cottage industry is no less important.

In the rural areas there are quite a large number of village and cottage industries operating in the state. Orissa has the glorious tradition of having artisan based units well spread all over the state. These industries need low capital investment and mostly use locally available resources. They are labour intensive units providing opportunities of self employment to rural people. In spite of the advantages claimed by these units, they mostly suffer from lack of finance. For which these units have continued to remain traditional. Efforts towards modernisation and renovation have not taken place significantly. The income of the rural artisans has remained low. They continued to remain below the poverty line. Hence, greater emphasis is placed upon the supply of finance by institutional financing agencies. In course of time, a wide spectrum of institutional financing agencies have come into existence in the state. The institutional financing agencies are Co-operative Banks, Commercial Banks, Regional Rural Banks and Orissa State Financial Corporation.

Since the nationalisation of Banks, there has taken place a phenomenal growth of institutional financing agencies in the state. Both in respect of geographical coverage and functional spread, the institutional financing agencies have shown a significant record of performance. With finance supplied from these sources, the rural artisans have made a dent in the development of artisans based units. It is against this background that an humble attempt is made to study the role of institutional financing agencies for the development and promotion of rural artisans in Orissa.

However, the study is primarily confined to Puri district where the artisan based units are largely concentrated. It is observed that there are nearly 4.2 lakh artisans in the state. Of the total workers engaged in various occupations, artisans account for nearly 3.2 per cent of the total in the year 1978. The number of artisans operating in Puri district alone account for 38 thousands. Of the total artisans, at the state level, the percentage share of artisans in Puri district was 9.2 per cent of the total in the aforesaid year. It is further revealing that bulk of these artisans are mostly located in the rural areas. It is further noticed that among the various categories of artisan based units located at the state, a sizeable number of these units are mostly found at the district level. Besides, it has certain categories of artisan based units which do not figure in other parts of the state. Moreover products of village and cottage industries, produced in Puri district, have great marketing prospects both in the country and outside the country. It is for all these reasons that the study is primarily confined to the district of Puri.

The district is at present covered by a number of institutional financing agencies like Co-operative Banks, Commercial Banks, RRBs and OSFC. Besides, there is also the regional office of KVIC in the district. Under different plans, and specially after nationalisation these institutional financing agencies have made significant improvements in financing the artisans, particularly the rural artisans.

The rural artisans have been categorised in the banking circle as the weaker sections. Besides, village and cottage industries have been included in the category of priority sectors for purpose of receiving special treatment. As per the guidelines issued by RBI, Banks are required to channelise 40 per cent of their total credit to designated priority sectors in which village and cottage industries form an important component. Of the total priority sector advances again nearly 25 per cent of the advances are earmarked for the weaker sections amongst the priority sector borrowers. Besides, Commercial Banks, other institutional financing agencies also are required to fulfil this prescribed norm by RBI. At the district level, therefore, institutional financing agencies mainly include; Co-operative Banks, Commercial Banks, Puri Gramya Bank and Orissa State Financial Corporation etc. It is in this context that a sincere attempt is made to study the role of institutional financing agencies for the development and promotion of rural artisans in Puri district.

Objectives of the Study

The study is broadly undertaken with the following objectives.

1. To identify the basic needs and requirements of rural artisans and to analyse how these needs and requirements are proposed to be met by institutional credit agencies.

2. To discuss the existing organisational credit structure and operational policies of institutional financing agencies pursued for rural artisans.

3. To study the performance and working of institutional financing agencies operating in the district.

4. To examine the demand for and supply of credit to rural artisans with a view to make an assessment of the size of credit gap. Besides, discussion will also be made on purpose-wise distribution and utilisation of credit by rural artisans.

5. To study the impact of institutional credit on the growth of output, income and employment by rural artisans.

6. To study the problems confronted by rural artisans and institutional credit agencies in course of their loan operations.

Methodology of the Study

The study is undertaken both with the help of secondary and primary sources of information and data. For secondary sources, reliance is heavily placed on available standard literature, journals, publications of institutional credit agencies, and Government reports and publications etc. For this, help of standard libraries and research centres have been relied upon.

For primary sources, a field study has been undertaken for the purpose. The operational procedure of the field study is mentioned below. The field study has been undertaken with the help of a questionnaire canvassed to 120 sample selected rural artisans for eliciting relevant information from them. Besides, officials of institutional credit agencies have also been interviewed personally to elicit their opinions on certain issues having bearing on the study.

The coverage of the study, as has been mentioned, was confined to the district of Puri in Orissa which incidentally is typical of possessing all varieties of artisan (cottage) industries in the state. The artisan industries in Orissa can broadly be divided into five broad categories like; (i) Khadi & Village Industries, (ii) Handloom Industry, (iii) Handicraft Units, (iv) Coir Works and (v) Sericulture. The district of Puri is credited with all the above categories except the sericulture enterprises which are confined to limited pockets in the state. The study was therefore confined to the first four categories.

These four categories constitute some sub-groups under them. Out of total number of 40 types of sub-classifications seen in the rural areas of the district, where the individual artisans are engaged in one or the other of these forty categories of industries, 10 types were chosen with due consideration to the objectives of the study. While choosing the types, the choice was not exactly random. But attempt was made to select the typical units which would meet the need of getting all the parameters relevant to the study. To that extent an element of purposiveness was woven into the study. The approach was not estimational but a diagnostic attempt.

A comparative statement of the total number of sub-types of artisan units available in the rural areas of the district, and the number of types selected for the study is given below:

	Category of Artisan Industries	*Number of sub-types reported in rural areas of the district*	*Number of sub-type selected*
(i)	Khadi & Village Industries	10	2
(ii)	Handloom	1	1
(iii)	Handicraft	28	6
(iv)	Coir Works	1	1
	Total	40	10

For each of the sub-type numbering 10, a single location or village where these units are mostly found was chosen purposively. The sub-types of artisan units with their name and place of study chosen under KVIC, handlooms, handicraft and coir works are given below:

Main Category	*Sub Classification*	*Location*
A. Khadi & Village Industries	(1) Pottery	Jinti
B. Handloom	(2) Bamboo Works	Khairpur
C. Handicraft	(3) Weaving	Banamalipur
	(4) Bell Metal	Balakati
	(5) Stone Carving	Konark
	(6) Applique	Pipili
	(7) Pattachitra	Raghurajpur
	(8) Papier Machie	Chandanpur
	(9) Beads Making	Ballavpur
D. Coir	(10) Coir Works	Bira Govindapur

Under each of the ten locations, there were roughly 940 artisan units are seen to be functioning. Out of these units who had availed of the institutional credit were sorted out, which comes out to be 480. Of the total number of artisan units availing Bank credit, in each village 25 to 30 per cent of the artisan units/borrowers are selected randomly for field study, which comes out to be 120. A comparative statement of number of artisans availing bank credit in each village and number of sample artisans selected at a random for field study has been given below:

	Type of Artisan Units	*Name of Village*	*No. of Artisans availing Bank credit*	*No. of artisans selected on random for field study (25-30 per cent)*
1	2	3	4	5
1.	Pottery	Jhinti	68	17
2.	Bamboo Works	Khairpur	36	9
3.	Weaving	Banamalipur	108	27

(Contd.)

1	2	3	4	5
4.	Bell Metal	Balakati	100	25
5.	Stone Carving	Konark	15	4
6.	Applique	Pipli	49	12
7.	Pattachitra	Raghurajpur	24	6
8.	Papier Machie	Chandanpur	16	4
9.	Beads Making	Ballavpur	40	10
10.	Coir Works	Birgovindapur	24	6
	Total	**480**	**120**	

The field study was conducted in January 1989. The results of the field survey were tabulated and analysed. The study was undertaken on undivided Puri district.

2

Place and Role of Rural Artisans in the Context of Rural Industrialisation

The Indian economy as well as the Orissa economy have always remained agrarian in nature. They have generally been termed as industrially backward. The economy being principally dominated by the primary sector has not given way to massive and wide spread industrialisation. Greater importance has always been given to the agricultural sector in all these years, since the launching of Five-Year-Plan in 1951. However, for attaining accelerated and self-sustained growth the development of both agricultural and industrial sectors was considered vital in the scheme of planning and development. Under the impetus of planning industrialisation received utmost attention during plan period. However, it is noticed that expansion of large and medium scale industries was quite phenomenal. The process of economic policy and planning persued both at the centre and in the state have encouraged the growth and expansion of large and medium industrial enterprises. These industries alone encountered for a sizeable bulk of investment meant for industrial sector. These industries are mostly established in big metropolis, cities and urban towns. It was initially thought by the planners that the establishment of large and medium scale enterprises in big cities and towns would help in transmitting the benefits of industrialisation into remote rural areas where they were mostly required. But in course of time it was noticed that the growth inducing impulses of industrialisation did not flow from cities and towns to rural areas where majority of the population in the country and at the state level lived. In other words the benefit of industrialisation did not percolate downwards to touch majority of population living in remote rural centres.

The rural areas thus remained isolated from the pace of industrialisation persued at the national level. However, at present greater thrust has been imposed for industrialising the rural areas through the development of rural industries like village and cottage industries. Moreover, these industries are mostly seen and practised in the rural households with traditional tools and implements. These industries however have got immense potentiality to provide immediate job opportunity at a low unit cost. Moreover, these units mostly produce products based on locally available resources. Against this background the importance and role of rural artisans engaged in various village and cottage industries have got relevance to be discussed.

Industrialisation in general is said to be an essential requirement for a rapid and self sustained development of an economy. While looking into the economic history of other industrially advanced countries of the world, it is envinced that the accelerated pace of economic development was mainly possible in these countries due to rapid industrialisation. It may be observed that the process of industrialising the economy was carried out in those countries with the expectation that this would help increasing national income and per capita income to a large extent. Besides, industrialisation would further help for a structural transformation of the economy, by which the economy will gradually switch over from primary to secondary sector and later to adopt a more developed tertiary sector. A structural shifting of this type thus not only solve certain inherent problems associated with the concept of growth and development but sets in motion a chain of activities by which the growth becomes a self propelling one.

The newly independent countries of Asia, Africa and Latin America have hoped to repeat the performance of the developed countries and become industrialised. However, it is noticed that their hopes have not been materialised and the weak industrial base adopted by the developing countries have rather deepened to push them farther off from the path of development.

The share of the industrial sector in the total GDP can be viewed as an important indicator of the level of industrialisation of a country or a region. In 1980 the proportion of total industrial output to the Gross Domestic product in the developing countries (minus India and China) was less than 20 per cent. This proportion was higher for India (26 per cent). China (47 per cent) and middle income countries (37 per cent). As against this, for the rest of other developing countries it was too low to have any perceptible impact on them. But however, the gross figures stated above are very much disturbing, when it is compared with that of numerous socio-economic problems faced by these countries. While examining their implications, for the vast majority of the poor living in rural areas of these countries, one can very well realise the limited role of industrialisation in these countries[1]. The limited role of industrialisation is also greatly noticed in the country like India. After so may years of planned economic development, her various regions are still out of the touch with industrialisation. As a result of this even today a bulk of its population is still depending on agriculture for their livelihood and occupation. It is not that structural shift is completely absent but the change is very thin and weak. So industrialisation and modernisation has not moved to the rural areas as desired. It is due to the fact that industrialisation, by and large, is being confined to large urban centres and tends to cater to the needs of only small urban elite groups. Furthermore, lack of capital, absence of trained manpower and entrepreneurship kept rural areas outside the purview of industrialisation. Rural industrialisation has, therefore been one of the major thrusts of many developing economies, including that of India.

Meaning of Rural Industrialisation

The word 'Rural Industrialisation' ordinarily means industrialising rural areas or developing industries in the rural areas. The concept of rural industrialisation, however, has been viewed from two perspective angles; firstly it may be termed as 'industrialisation in rural areas' and secondly, it may be termed as 'industrialisation of rural area'.

The first category, which is termed as 'industrialisation in rural areas' is a programmatic approach. It puts emphasis on the type of industry which can be developed or dispersed under the available factors of production and market condition prevailing in the rural areas. It mostly presupposes establishment of (i) large industries, which use agricultural products as their raw materials, (ii) artisan units which are mostly traditional, and (iii) small scale units which undertake processing agricultural products. It shows that industrialisation in rural areas in often characterised by straight jacket national programmes and even international programmes.

In the second category which is termed as 'industrialisation of rural areas', a greater emphasis is put on industrialising the rural areas. Rural industrialisation here is treated as a subprocess as well as a means to diversify and modernise the rural economy. Flexibility and development need oriented strategy are the hall mark of this perspective. It laid emphasis on industrialisation as a means to develop the rural areas. Thus, it requires a systematic change and intervention into the prevailing structure to promote rural industrialisation. And the structure differ from country to country and region to region. Accordingly the rural industries which are required to be developed also differ from country to country and from region to region[2].

It may be noted that for making the rural areas industrialised, it is not very much reliable to depend on the first type of straight-jacket programmes. It is due to the fact that a bulk of the people living in rural areas are unskilled and are not able to engage themselves in modern type of industries started in rural areas. Furthermore, it is not very much easy to change the technological level of these industries to suit to the moods of these rural people. Again the skill of rural people can not be so upgraded overnight to meet the modernisation needs. On this background, the 'industrialisation of the rural areas' seems to be more relevant.

Typology of Rural Industry

Rural industries have been defined differently in different countries and from region to region. However, classification in general is mostly made on the basis of capital and labour invested. In case of India rural industries mostly mean village and cottage industrial units which constitute the lowest category under small scale industrial units.

Small scale ancillary units, one of the important type of small scale units are generally engaged in manufacturing parts, components, sub-assemblies, tooling or intermediaries and supplying or proposing to supply 50 per cent of their production of the total service as the case may be to other units of production. Besides, according to present yardstick these units are also required to make an investment in plant and machinery upto Rs. 75.0 lakh in total. However, the industrial units making an investment in plant and machinery upto Rs. 60 lakh are treated as small scale industrial units. The enhancement of investment limit from Rs. 7.5 lakh to Rs. 10.0 lakh was made effective from 1978 and to Rs. 20 lakh from 1980 and further to the limit of Rs. 35 lakh from the year 1985. In 1991 this limit was further enhanced to Rs. 45 lakhs and that of ancillaries to Rs. 55 lakh.

Again tiny units which constitute another variant are those units of small units which are mostly located in villages and towns with a population not exceeding 50,000 and whose original investment in plant and machinery does not exceed Rs. 5 lakhs. As against this, village and cottage industries which constitute the smallest form of small scale industries are defined to mean activity of artisans irrespective of location) or of small units (viz. manufacturing, processing preservation and servicing) in villages and small towns with population not exceeding 50,000, involving utilisation of locally available natural resources and / or human skills and where individual credit requirements do not exceed Rs. 25,000.[3]

It is observed that the Government of India has put greater emphasis on the development of artisan based village and cottage industrial units in the country. The meaning and definition of various categories of industries as mentioned above are found explicit expression in the industrial policy resolutions announced from time to time by the Central Government in general and the State Governments in particular. As such, village and cottage industries broadly includes industries in the category of Khadi and Village Industries, Handlooms, Handicrafts, Coir and Sericulture. The characteristics features of these units are that they are mostly located in the rural or semi urban areas, mostly use locally available resources, and need low capital investment, and do not require high and sophisticated technology etc. It is a fact to note that the term called rural industry may also include some other type of industrial activities. However, for purpose of this study the artisan units as mentioned above and again making investment upto Rs. 25,000 towards meeting their credit needs are only considered.

Need for Rural Industrialisation

Industrialisation of the rural areas is required, at present, for multifarious reasons. The most important among them is that industrialisation in the rural areas, seems to be mostly fitting into the new concept of 'growth point' theory. In the context of our economy the theory basically mean developing the economy at the grassroot level and village level.

The 'growth point' model envisages a four tier system of growth strategy. Under the system the growth process is required to be mooted from the village level, which may very well be termed as 'service centres'. Service centres are at the lowest level, and are centres of activity serving a population of 5 thousands to 10 thousands, concentrated in one village or dispersed in a number of villages or hamlets. These are called Service Centres in the sense that they possess certain service centres in the form of custom services, community centres and government functionaries. The long term objective of these 'Service Centres' is to create channels, through which urban growth inducing impulses can penetrate into the remotest part of the country. Development of these centres will generate external and internal economies of the scale. In the next level, in the hierarchy there are 'growth points'. Growth points are very much crucial points and they may lie between ten to twenty service points. The development of growth point will generate economic activity in the local areas and will create a situation where a sizeable portion of rural population which is swelling into the urban slums of the large cities, can be absorbed. In the third stage of the growth programme, there are 'growth centres'. The population of these centres may vary between 50 thousand and 5 lakhs on an average. But their impact will be felt by large sections of population ranging between 10 lakhs to 20 lakhs. These growth centres are mostly functioning for five to ten growth points. These centres will possess manufacturing or secondary activity as their principal activity. These growth centres are thus full grown urban centres. At the apex of the growth strategy there exists the 'growth poles', which serve a population ranging between 5 lakh and 25 lakh. These growth poles have got the capacity of disseminating financial, technological, research and industrial impulses to all the centres and points within areas of their operation.[4]

According to the model both internal and external forces are required to function in harmony for the growth of the area. The internal forces will be generated by the available entrepreneurs who are capable of undertaking any industrial activities. External forces, however, operate out of the availability of infrastructure facilities, which are existing or will be supplied with plan efforts. The two forces functioning effectively will lead a climate of growth, which will change the stagnant and semi-stagnant rural economy, to a dynamic growth path. The growth thus achieved in the service centres and growth points will create two types of spread effects. Primarily, it will improve the socio-economic condition of the rural areas and the people living therein. Simultaneously, being developed internally it will also help in supplementing the growth and development of urban centres, growth centres and the growth poles. Thus, it will create linkages both backward and forward. In this way there will happen a two way flow of developmental activities from service centres towards growth poles and from growth pole towards service centres.

This type of interaction can only be achieved if industrial activities in the rural areas will be properly activated and encouraged. This responsibility may not be shifted to agriculture. Because of continuous pressure of labour force in agriculture, the sector has been overcrowded with surplus manpower. So the ultimate solution lies with developing and protecting the rural industries in this regard.

It may be emphasised that the purpose of industrialisation in rural areas is to carry out the message of modernisation to the villages and stimulate their social and economic progress. For the purpose the candidate centres or growth points for the rural industrialisation should be so chosen that the effects of modernisation could easily radiate to villages lying on the periphery within a given radius. Such centres may be well equipped with infrastructural facilities to certain extent, so that it will provide enough external economies to help reducing industrial costs to the minimum and yet bring the benefits of industrialisation to a majority of rural population. Thus industrialisation of the growth centres supported by surrounding villages could in turn support the socio-economic transformation and modernisation of the latter by effectively radiating spread effects. By the same manner the industrial activity in growth points will support developed industrial towns and cities and will be benefited from radiation of the latter's spread effects and modernisation. It thus shows that rural industrialisation has got capacity to break the problem of unbalanced growth. And moreover, it will create a situation where various areas will be developed simultaneously, in terms of supporting and sustaining one another's economic activity and social and economic development on the basis of local multiplier and radiation effect.

Besides this, the rural industrialisation is also required for the purpose of reducing continuous pressure on agriculture. In the state as well as in the country, a bulk of the population lives in rural areas and depend upon agriculture for their livelihood. In such a situation the economic development of a region as a whole will not be improved unless the rural income and employment are improved in a substantial manner, in a short span of time, and this can only be done through the development of rural industries. If we look to economic history of other industrially advanced countries of the world, then it is clear that their economic development has only been achieved through industrialisation. Furthermore, industrialisation is carried out in those countries in such a manner that national income and per capita income have increased significantly. Besides, structure of the economy has also undergone transformation. It has gradually switched over from primary sector to secondary sector; and then to tertiary sector. However in almost all the developing countries, agriculture continues to remain as the mainstay of the majority population who mostly live in the rural areas. It is true that in the recent years the percentage share of secondary and tertiary sector in the total Gross Domestic Product have increased compared to that of the agriculture. Yet the latter still continues to be the major sector in the economy. It is in this background that a suggestion for the development of rural industries is often made. It is not that structural shift is completely absent but the change is slow and thin. There is the need for persuading entrepreneurs to start industries in the countryside.

Rural industrialisation generally leads to urbanisation of the rural areas. It is said that industrialisation and urbanisation go hand in hand. Urbanisation leads to a situation where the people generally become more efficient economically. The well developed social and economic infrastrure help them to develop their innovative and creative outlook towards better production. But the fact is that the pace of urbanisation is very much slow in the country as well as in the state. Till today only about 11.8 per cent of the entire population are seen to be living in urban areas of the state. As a result, a major portion of the country's population has not been influenced by the socio-economic changes, which have occurred with industrialisation and urbanisation. But it is very much required that the process of industrialisation and urbanisation should move to the suitable growth centres around villages. considering the preponderance of the agricultural and rural sectors, the structural shift should be promoted through intensive efforts of developing village or rural industries.

Rural industries not only leads to urbanisation, but also it has got a greater role in reducing the dualistic nature of the economy. As stated earlier the process of urabnisation and industrialisation is mostly concentrated in the urban areas. As a result of which a dual economy is seen to be existing. In one side there are sophisticated industries, high technological investment and ultra modern life style etc., which are confined to cities and metropolis. As against this there are poverty, lack of civic amenities, lack of proper facilities of health and sanitation, and traditional industries using tools and implements operating in the rural areas. This type of dual economy is generally responsible for continuing development stimuli in a few cities and towns while keeping a vast majority of population living in rural areas to remain out of its reach. It aggravates the centre peripheral conflict and thereby stands in the way of optimum allocation of resources. To solve this problem, creation of large scale employment opportunities in the rural areas is very much required. For this purpose development of rural industries seems to be the only feasible solution.

Moreover to have a sustained growth rate in the economy, the necessity of developing industries located in rural areas is quite essential. Originally the growth strategy was on development of heavy and large scale industries, with the main purpose of import substitution. But it is noticed that these industries have ultimately led to inflationary situation, shortage of essential commodities, continuous balance of payment crisis, concentration of infrastructure in cities and negligence of rural sectors. Accordingly the planners have shifted their priorities, in favour of the agricultural sectors, since later part of the Third Five-Year Plan. The introduction of 'green revolution' has made the agricultural sector more important, by solving the food problem of the country[5]. But due to frequent visit of natural calamities the income and employment generation has faced a set back in the agricultural sector. The national income also showed a vast amplitude of fluctuations from year to year depending on the performance of the agricultural sector. This resulted in pulling down the long term growth rate of the country to a considerable extent. So it is noticed that greater dependence on large scale industries and on agriculture has not helped in enhancing the growth rate of the country. The long term growth rate as a whole has never remained above 3.5 per cent per annum. With 2 per cent of annual population growth rate, the actual growth rate of the economy has remained only at 1.5 per cent per annum. So in this context, one may feel that when food problem is already under control due to the introduction of green revolution, the priority for a sustained growth rate is to be achieved at the desired rate. For this purpose an integrated development of rural areas, through a complementary growth of agriculture and industry, is mostly required. For the purpose the promotion of artisan based rural industries seems to achieve the desired solution.

Besides, all these rural based village and cottage industrial units are also required for the implementation of government level special programmes for the benefit of lower income group living in the rural areas in a better manner. These programmes include Small Farmers Development Agency (SFDA), Marginal Farmers and Agricultural Labours Development Agencies (MFAL), Drought Prone Area Programme (DPAP) and Tribal Development Agency (TDA) etc. Though expenditure on these programmes have increased under various plans yet their impact on weaker sections is not very much encouraging. A World Bank Study made in 1977 shows that identification of small farmers were mostly faulty and supply of credit to them was not covering the entire credit need of these farmers. This resulted in poor recovery of loan and mounting overdues on borrowers etc. All these programmes are observed to be in the nature of palliatives rather than correctives. They are certainly useful for helping the weaker sections but their relevance could be further enhanced if a well designed rural industrialisation programme could be conceived and developed for adoption.

Furthermore, artisan units which constitute an important segment of rural industries are required to be developed in the sense that, they will help to promote the growth of both the sectors like agriculture and industry, simultaneously. Development of rural industries is very important to install a dynamic change in both agricultural and industrial sector. In the first place, expansion of industries at the village level requires more agro-based raw materials, which will ultimately lead to more production, price stability and increase in the living standard of the people. Secondly, industrialisation is required to have certain strong forward and backward linkages. As a result of which a given volume of investment would make a far greater dynamic chain multiplier impact on output, income and employment, in the rural areas as well as outside of it.

It is also fact that due to larger application of mechanisation in agriculture there will be some displacement of workers from farm sector. For employment of these displaced persons village and cottage industries appears to be the only hope. It is further estimated that the labour absorption capacity of the agricultural sector in general is going down. Nearly 75 per cent of the population of the country was depending upon agriculture for their occupation earlier. Now the proportion has gone down to 68 per cent according to 1981 Census. It is estimated in future the proportion will still go down. With the increase in number of population the labour absorbing capacity of the agricultural sector is not increasing. It is also estimated that percentage of labour force on non formal sector may increase from the existing level of 10 per cent to 30 per cent in the coming two or three decade. In this context the role of rural industries becomes more important for providing alternative avenues of employment to rural labour force.

Development of rural industries is essential for checking exodus of rural population from rural centres to cities and urban towns. When rural population migrate to urban areas it creates socio-economic problem. It results in the growth of informal sector. There is congestion, mushroom growth of slums and insanitation. To solve these problems, industrialisation in the rural areas need be undertaken in a vigorous scale. For this rural industries in the form of village and cottage industries constitute an ideal alternative of employing labour in a large scale and of generating higher income and improving the standard of living of the rural poor.

As stated earlier, the artisan units coming under the category of Khadi & Village Industries, Handlooms, Handicrafts, Sericulture and Coir constituting the most important form of rural industries, are seen to be operating in the country as well as in the state. A bulk of the rural population is engaged in these trade not only at present but from age old times. It is noticed that these units provide the large number of employment opportunities after that of agriculture.

Needs and Aspirations of Rural Artisans

The growth and promotion of these artisan units greatly depends upon fulfilment of their needs and requirements. It is noticed that persons engaged in the village and cottage industries generally live in rural areas, which mostly lack proper infrastructural social and commercial facilities. In case the infrastructural facilities will be developed then the spread effect from urban areas will move to these areas and socio-economic transformation of the village and artisan units can be attained.

Another most important requirement for their development is the provision of proper education and training facilities, which should be of functional and technical type in nature. Mostly non-traditional type of training programmes will be of immense help to the artisans.

The rural artisan units generally are of labour intensive in nature. They use simple indigenous technology for their unit. But certain innovative and new technology should be developed which will generate more production and side by side will not be labour displacing in nature.

Growth and promotion of artisan units further requires marketing of their product at the institutional level. It will make them free from the clutches of traders and middlemen etc.

Artisan units also requires easy supply of raw material. Raw materials which they use are mostly resources which are locally available. Due to reasons like afforestation and environment protection, these resources are going to be out of reach for them. So supply of raw materials from institutional sources will promote their trade.

Besides all these, finance is the most important requirement of the artisans. Artisans are mostly poor and face dearth of resources to undertake investment. They are mostly trapped in a vicious circle of low production, low income and inadequate investment[6]. To break this deadlock sufficient resources need be channelised to the artisan sector by various institutional credit agencies operating in the country and in the state. However, the All-India Debt Investment Survey conducted by RBI in 1971 shows that of the total financing made available to the artisan sector in the state 7.4 per cent was supplied by the institutional agencies. As against this 92.6 per cent of the assistance was obtained from non-institutional sources. It shows that there is greater need for financing the artisan sector from institutional sources.[7]

It may be observed that for the development of rural artisans, finance is necessary but this may not be the only essential condition. Along with finance, the rural artisans need certain complementary assistance like marketing, storage, supply of inputs through retail channels at reasonable price, training and guidance and above all patronage by government and semi-government organisations for furthering their trade. Keeping all these in mind the government of India, in collaboration with the state governments has promoted so many financial institutions, organisations, agencies, and boards, for this purpose. These institutions not only provide finance but also provide assistance in the form of marketing, technological improvement, supplying of raw materials, custom services, training and guidance. The government has set up All India agencies like Khadi and Village Industries Commission, All India Handloom Board, All India Handicraft Board, Central Silk Board and Coir Board etc. which are mostly promotional in nature. In the state level government has set up Orissa State Handicraft Corporation, State Handloom Development Corporation and etc. for this purpose.

Apart from these boards and agencies various programmes have also been started by the government for the growth and promotion of rural industries. One such programme is the Rural Industries programme, which was started in 1962-63. Under the programme Central Government provided 100 per cent grant to meet the establishment cost and entrepreneurs were given loan at the rate of 5.5 per cent per annum. The projects however, could not succeed for long due to lack of proper marketing facilities and inadequate training facility in the rural centres etc. DICs (District Industries Centres) were set up in May 1978. This replaced erstwhile Rural Industries Project Programmes. Out of 415 districts it covered nearly 410 districts of the country. It thus acts as a promotional centre looking into the overall needs of the rural artisans. Integrated Rural Development Programme (IRDP) was formulated later to render more direct benefit to the rural artisans living in countryside. Under the scheme 600 poorest families including that of artisans are required to be identified and helped each year, in each Block, during the Sixth Five-Year Plan. Among these families 100 families would be assisted through the village and cottage industries and another 100 families through rural service activities. It was estimated that during Sixth Plan Period around 25 lakhs of families would be covered under village and cottage industries and an equal number in rural service sector.

Growth and promotion of rural artisans must form an important policy objective in any scheme of developmental plan. The occupation in traditional no doubt but it has a large bearing on the growth of the economy. They contribute positively towards the generation of output, income and employment in the economy. These artisans, who are hitherto neglected, need be encouraged to join the main stream of development. In their efforts towards contributing for development, the rural artisans, however, come across with certain problems. Of the problems met by rural artisans, lack of finance is identified as one of the main bottlenecks. Consequently, supply of finance through institutional sources is considered more plausible. Since nationalisation of banks in the year 1969 till the present time a wide spectrum of institutional credit agencies have come into existence in the state in general and Puri district in particular. Over the years, liberal financing by institutional credit agencies has helped rural artisans to grow in number. Besides, various promotional measures by institutional credit agencies and other developmental agencies have also been followed for the upliftment of rural artisans. It is against this background that an humble attempt is made to study the role of institutional financing agencies for the development and promotion of rural artisans in Orissa with particular reference to district of Puri.

REFERENCES

1. Srinivas Y. Thakur, *Rural Industrialisation in India*, Sterling Publishing Pvt. Ltd., New Delhi, 1985.
2. R.P. Mishra, *Rural Industrialisation in Third World Countries*, Sterling Publishing Pvt. Ltd., New Delhi, 1985.
3. Bank of India, Head Office, C.B. Division, Community Banking Part I, Revised Schemes of Financing Assistance to SSI.
4. Srinivas Y. Thakur, *op. cit.*
5. S.N. Bhattacharya, *Rural Industrialisation in India*, B.R. Publishing Corporation, Delhi, 1980.
6. S.N. Mishra, *Growth of Commercial Banking in Orissa*, Anu Books, Meerut, 1984.
7. L.K. Naidu, *Bank Finance for Rural Artisans*, Asish Publishing House, New Delhi, 1988.

3

Rural Economic Backdrop and Current Economic Status of Rural Artisans

ORISSA

In the previous chapter an attempt has been made to analyse the role of rural artisans in the context of rural industrialisation, for attaining higher level of economic development. Accordingly the primary focus of this chapter is to make an indepth review of the rural economic background of Orissa in general and Puri district in particular. Besides, an attempt is also made to discuss the current socio-economic status of the rural artisans in the state, and the district respectively. Furthermore, in this chapter an attempt is made to analyse and identify the various needs and aspirations of the rural artisans. In the light of these discussions an humble effort is made to study as to what extent, the institutional credit agencies can undertake the task of fulfilling these needs and aspirations of the rural artisans.

Growth of Income

Economic feature of the state is characterised by low level of state as well as per capita income. Available data, calculated on the basis of 1970-71 prices reveals that the total Net State Domestic Product of the state has increased from Rs. 10.52 crores in 1970-71 to Rs. 17.04 crores in 1988-89. Table 3.1 reveals that over the period the state's income has increased by 62.0 per cent, and the annual growth rate of the state income between 1970-71 and 1988-89 was 3.5 per cent on an average per annum.

Table 3.1

Net State Domestic Product at Factor Cost in Orissa, 1970-71 to 1988-89

(Rs. in crores)

Year	*At current prices*	*Percentage increase (+) or decrease (-) over the previous year*	*At 1970-71 prices*	*Percentage increase (+) or decrease (-) over the previous year*
(1)	(2)	(3)	(4)	(5)
1970-71	10.52	–	10.52	–
1971-72	10.62	1.0	9.53	(-)9.4
1972-73	13.10	23.4	10.66	10.7
1973-74	16.21	23.7	11.22	6.3
1974-75	16.92	4.4	9.68	(-)13.7
1975-76	17.60	4.0	11.48	18.3
1976-77	16.92	(-) 3.8	10.67	(-)6.9
1977-78	21.11	24.7	12.58	17.9
1978-79	22.17	5.0	13.40	6.5
1979-80	22.50	1.5	11.24	(-)6.2
1980-81	30.96	37.6	12.57	11.4
1981-82	35.61	15.3	12.71	1.6
1982-83	36.00	1.0	12.08	(-)5.5
1983-84	48.10	33.9	14.93	24.2

(Contd.)

(1)	(2)	(3)	(4)	(5)
1984-85	47.41	(-) 1.6	13.59	(-)8.9
1985-86	56.53	19.2	15.69	15.4
1986-87	59.37	5.0	15.70	0.1
1987-88	61.52	3.6	14.85	(-)5.4
1988-89	73.60	19.6	17.04	15.1
Average Annual growth rate between 1970-71 and 1988-89		12.0		3.5

Source: Government of Orissa, P & C Department, Economic Survey 1989-90, Cutack, 1990, PP, A1 & A2.

The sectoral composition of the state income reveals that a major portion of the total state income is being derived from the primary sector, where agriculture constitutes an important segment. Calculated at 1970-71 Constant Prices, it is noticed from Table 3.2 that the primary sector in the year 1970-71 has accounted for nearly 66.3 per cent of the total state income of Orissa, where as the secondary sector and tertiary sector accounted for nearly 10.2 and 23.5 per cent respectively. In the year 1988-89, however, the percentage share of primary sector to the total state income declined to 61.5 per cent, according to 1970-71 prices.

As against this, the percentage share of secondary sector and tertiary sector to the total state income was 9.8 and 28.7 per cent respectively, in the aforesaid reference year. This gives an indication, that over the years, percentage share of primary sector in the total state income whereas declined, the percentage share of secondary and tertiary sector in the total state income showed a marked improvement. This is mainly due to the reason that over the plan periods, greater emphasis was put on for the expansion of secondary and tertiary sector, compared to the primary sector in the state's economy.

Table 3.2

Sectorwise Net State Domestic Product of Orissa at Factor Cost at 1970-71 Prices

(Rs. in crores)

Sl. No.	*Sectors*	*1970-71*	*1980-81*	*1988-89*
1.	Primary Sector – Agriculture, Animal Husbandry, Forestry, Fishing, Mining & Quarrying.	698.13 (66.3)	796.70 (63.7)	1050.16 (61.5)
2.	Secondary Sector – Industry, Construction, Electricity	107.58 (10.2)	128.81 (10.3)	167.62 (9.8)
3.	Tertiary Sector –			
	(a) Transport Communication, Trade, Storage etc.	118.35 (11.3)	144.60 (11.5)	203.94 (11.9)
	(b) Services (Banking and Insurances, Real estate, Public Administration, Other services, etc.)	128.21 (12.2)	181.07 (14.5)	286.97 (16.8)
4.	Net Domestic Product at factor cost	1,052.27 (100)	1,251.18 (100)	1,708.69 (100)

Source: Government of Orissa P & C Department, *Economic Survey* (1989-90), Cuttack, 1991, PP, A.4.

Per Capita Income

Per capita income is also very low in the state. Calculated on the basis of 1970-71 prices, per capita income of Orissa, whereas stood at Rs. 485.0 in the year 1970-71, the same increased to Rs. 566.0 to the year 1988-89. It is evident from the Table 3.3 that the per capita income over the years has increased only at the rate of 1.5 per cent per annum.

Table 3.3

Per Capita Net State Domestic Product in Orissa 1970-71 and 1988-89 (At Current and Constant Prices)

Year	*At current prices (in Rs.)*	*Percentage increase (±) or decrease over the previous year*	*At 1970-71 prices (in Rs.)*	*Percentage increase (±) or decrease over the previous year*
1970-71	484.98	–	484.98	–
1971-72	478.33	(-) 1.4	429.64	(-) 11.4
1972-73	577.95	20.8	465.67	8.4
1973-74	701.21	21.3	485.57	4.3
1974-75	716.50	2.2	410.13	(-) 15.5
1975-76	730.89	2.0	475.72	16.0
1976-77	686.83	(-) 5.6	434.84	(-) 8.6
1977-78	845.00	22.5	503.64	15.8
1978-79	872.41	3.2	527.46	4.5
1979-80	871.51	(-) 0.1	435.19	(-) 17.5
1980-81	1181.12	35.5	477.36	9.7
1981-82	1339.73	13.4	477.24	(-) 0.01
1982-83	1327.59	(-) 0.9	443.18	(-) 7.1
1983-84	1744.95	31.4	540.51	22.0
1984-85	1685.54	(-) 3.4	483.21	(-) 10.6
1985-86	1973.45	17.4	547.70	13.3
1986-87	2035.87	3.2	538.43	(-) 1.7
1987-88	2972.97	1.8	500.26	(-) 7.1
1988-89	2437.65	17.6	565.90	13.1
Average Annual growth rate between 1970-71 and 1988-89		10.7		1.5

Source: Government of Orissa, P & C Department, *Economic Survey*, 1989-90, Cuttack, 1991, PP, A1 & A2.

The statewise distribution of per capita income as shown in Table 3.4 indicates that there is a great deal of disparity, between the per capita income of Orissa and other states of the country. Looking at the 1970-71 price index it is noticed that per capita income of Orissa stood at Rs. 477 and Rs. 500 in the year 1980-81 and 1987-88 respectively. During this period per capita income at the all India level stood at Rs. 698 and Rs. 893 respectively. This indicates that per capita income of Orissa stands at 68.3 and 56.0 per cent of the total per capita income at the all India level.

Table 3.4

Per Capita Net State Domestic Product of Different States (At current prices and at 1970-71 prices)

(in Rs.)

Sl. No.	*States*	*At current prices*		*AT 1970-71 prices*	
		1980-81	*1987-88*	*1980-81*	*1987-88*
1.	Andhra Pradesh	1358	2653	647	1495
2.	Assam	1221	2335	558	655
3.	Bihar	934	1904	441	472
4.	Gujarat	1968	3636	904	853
5.	Haryana	2351	4214	1060	2572
6.	Jammu & Kashmir	1455	–	642	–
7.	Karnatak	1454	2802	687	776
8.	Kerala	1385	2598	621	1386
9.	Madhya Pradesh	1183	2404	517	633
10.	Maharashtra	2244	4490	957	1159
11.	Orissa	1181	2073	477	500
12.	Punjab	2620	5477	1354	1755
13.	Rajsthan	1224	2326	537	583
14.	Tamil Nadu	1324	2980	584	915
15.	Uttar Pradesh	1272	2488	519	1486
16.	West Bengal	1643	3193	797	898
	All India	1631	2848	698	893

Source : Government of Orissa, P & C Department, *Economic Survey*, 1989-90, Cuttack, 1991, PP, A.6 and A.7.

Disparity in Per Capita Income

There is also wide disparity in per capita income between Orissa and all India. It is revealed from the Table 3.5 that the gap in per capita income, whereas stood at 23.8 per cent in 1970-71, the same increased to 26.7 per cent in the year 1988-89. This indicates that the performance of the state's economy is not very much encouraging.

Table 3.5

Per Capita Net State Domestic Product and Per Capita Net National Product at Factor Cost at 1970-71 Prices

(in Rs.)

Years	*Per capita NSDP Orissa*	*Per Capita NNP India*	*Gap in Rs.*	*Gap in % to All India figure (col.4 as % to Col.3)*
1	2	3	4	5
1970-71	482.4	632.8	150.4	23.8
1971-72	434.1	626.6	192.5	30.7
1972-73	565.6	604.1	147.5	24.4
1973-74	480.7	621.2	140.5	22.6
1974-75	426.8	617.6	190.8	30.9
1975-76	489.8	663.6	173.8	26.2
1976-77	420.9	659.2	238.3	36.1
1977-78	500.4	701.0	200.6	28.5
1978-79	514.5	727.8	213.1	29.3
1979-80	435.2	677.8	242.6	35.8
1980-81	477.0	698.0	221.0	31.7
1981-82	477.2	636.8	241.6	37.9
1982-83	443.2	614.1	171.1	27.9

(Contd.)

1	2	3	4	5
1983-84	540.5	683.8	143.3	21.0
1984-85	483.0	775.0	292.0	37.7
1985-86	548.0	798.0	250.0	31.3
1986-87	538.0	820.0	282.0	34.4
1987-88	500.0	893.0	393.0	44.0
1988-89	566.0	772.2	206.2	26.7

Source: (1) 1970-71, to 1980, Government of Orissa, P & C department, The Economic Base of Orissa for the Sixth Plan, 1980-85, Cuttack, PP, 4.

(2) 1980-89, Government of Orissa, P & C department, *Economic Survey*, 1989-90, Cuttack, 1990, PP, A1, AM, A.8.

Population

The state of Orissa has experienced a high rate of population growth over the last few decades. According to the Census report conducted for the year 1961, 1971 and 1981, the total population has been calculated to be 175, 219 and 264 lakhs respectively. The annual growth rate of population in the state between 1961 and 1971, and between 1971 and 1981 was 2.5 and 2.0 per cent respectively.

Available data show that of the total, population, 133 lakhs are males and 131 lakhs are females. In terms of percentage the proportion of male population to the total whereas stood at 50.4 per cent the same was 49.7 per cent in case of females. According to the 1981 census, Scheduled Caste and Scheduled Tribe population taken together accounts for 37.1 per cent of the total population compared to 23.5 per cent at the national level. Again among the total S.C. and S.T. population of the state, nearly 90.0 per cent of them live in the rural areas alone. The literacy rate in Orissa is not very much encouraging. As per 1981 census the state is having a literacy rate of 34.2 per cent compared to 36.2

per cent at the all India level. It is further observed that a sizeable section of the population in the state lives in the rural areas. According to 1981 census, 232 lakhs of population live in rural areas whereas only 32 lakhs of population live in urban areas. In percentage terms 88 per cent of the total population live in rural areas.[1]

In the year 1981, 122 lakhs and 142 lakhs are coming under the category of working and non working population respectively. In percentage terms, the share of working population to the total population constitutes 32.7 per cent. Again, of the total working population 86.35 lakhs are main workers who are fully employed and 13.57 lakhs are the marginal workers who are underemployed. It is further observed that a majority of the working population are found to be engaged in primary sector. According to 1981 census, sector-wise distribution of main workers show that in primary, secondary and tertiary sector nearly 77.9, 8.1 and 14.0 per cent of the total working population are engaged respectively. The distribution of main workers further reveals that of the total main workers 46.9 per cent are cultivators, 27.8 per cent are agricultural labourers, 3.3 per cent are household industrial workers and 22.0 per cent are other workers.[2]

Unemployment and Underemployment

As stated earlier a large proportion of state's population is non workers. Again out of the total working population, a sizeable portion remains underemployed or seasonally employed. The 38th round of N.S.S. (1983-84) has estimated about the projected unemployment position of the state for March 1989. It is estimated that, chronically unemployed persons and underemployed persons are estimated to be 1.9 lakhs and 10.3 lakhs respectively in the state. Data also shows that out of the total number of chronically unemployed and underemployed persons in the state, 1.07 lakh and 8.85 lakh respectively are to be seen in rural areas. In terms of percentage 55.1 per cent of the total unemployed in the state, and 86.0 per cent of the total underemployed in the state are to be seen in rural areas. So unemployment, underemployment and seasonal employment has become a regular feature in the rural areas of the state.

To solve these problems, creation of sufficient job opportunities is required. But it is noticed that the organised sector has got limited scope to provide employment facilities. In the unorganised sector, agriculture has already been over-crowded, so it is not in a position to absorb the surplus labour force and the new entrants to labour force. So greater importance is required to be given by the government on other unorganised industrial activities like village and cottage industries which have got a large potential for creating self employment in the rural areas.

Poverty Syndrome

It is noticed that quite a large section of the population in the state are poor and they live below the poverty line. It is noticed that by the year end of 1983-84 the state had 42.8 per cent of the total population living below the poverty line as compared to all India level of 37.4 per cent. It is further revealed that nearly 44.8 per cent of the rural population and 29.3 per cent of urban population in the state are found to be lying below the poverty line, on the basis of the per capita consumption expenditure. As against this, nearly 40 per cent of the rural population and 28.1 per cent of the urban population are lying below the poverty line at the all India level in the above mentioned reference year. This clearly indicates that persons living below the poverty line are more concentrated in rural areas of Orissa than at the all India level.

It is further seen that, whereas in the year 1970, the disparity in per capita monthly consumption expenditure between rural and urban areas was Rs. 23.89, the same increased to Rs. 103.15 in 1986. On account of this disparity, the incidence of poverty is found to be more deep seated in rural centres, compared to urban centres. Again, the concentration of poverty is greater amongst agricultural labourers and marginal farmers. Both of them account for nearly 42 per cent and 35 per cent respectively of the total population living below the poverty line in rural areas.

Low Asset Base

It is seen that a majority of the rural population do not possess adequate assets. As per the findings of the RBI the bottom 30 per cent of the rural families own only 4 to 5 per cent of the total rural assets. As against this, the top 30 per cent own nearly 80 per cent of the rural assets. Thus it clearly indicates a picture of skewed distribution of assets between different groups in the rural areas. RBI study further reveals that the proportion of assetless agricultural labourers has gone up from 17.2 per cent in 1961 to 29.0 per cent in 1981.[3]

Agriculture

Agriculture is the key sector of the economy. Two out of every three persons are directly dependent on agriculture for their livelihood. Contribution of this sector to the State Domestic Product is of nearly 50 per cent and the sector provides productive employment to about 67 per cent of the total work force. In 1988-89, of the total 15,540 thousand hectares of geographical area, the gross cropped area in percentage term constitutes nearly 59 per cent of the total. In percentage terms the share of net area sown to total gross cropped area in the state is of 68.5 per cent. It is also observed that nearly 70 per cent of net area sown under cultivation has to depend upon the mercy of the monsoon, which is always uncertain.

Foodgrains production is the principal motive of production in the State. In percentage term the area under food grains production to the total area under production constitutes, 83.5 per cent in the year 1987-88. So also the share of foodgrains to total agricultural production stood at 74.1 per cent in the year 1987-88. Rice is the major food crop grown in the state. In the year 1988-89 the area under rice to the total area under food grains, and the production of rice to the total production of foodgains constitute 53.2 and 68.4 per cent respectively. However its yield wentdown from 10.26 quintals per hectare in 1980-81 to 8.26 quintals per hectare in 1987-88. Besides food crops, production of non food crops has started showing an increasing trend. Available data show that the percentage share of total area under non-food crop, to the total cropped area has increased, from 22.6 per cent in 1980-81 to 26.6 per cent in 1987-88. The percentage share of total non-food crop production, to that of total production has also increased, from 19.9 per cent in 1980-81 to 25.8 per cent in the year 1987-88.[4]

Declining yield rate in foodgrains production and insignificant increase in the yield rate of non-food grains, reveal the characteristic features of the general low productivity of agriculture prevailing in the state. This is mainly due to the factors like lack of regular monsoon, lack of proper irrigation, lower percentage of area covered under high yielding varieties of seeds, low consumption of fertisliser, poor farm mechanisation and low land-man ratio etc. It is imperative here to state that dependence on risk prone, monsoon based agriculture may be minimised, through creation of massive employment potential in the rural non-farm sector, or in other words through rural based industrial activities.

Industry

It is on account of all these above mentioned factors that more stress is put on the development of industry in the state. At present the contribution of industries to the state income is very low. It is noticed that till the end of the July 1989 the state was having a total number of 219 large and medium scale industries with a capital investment of Rs. 100.85 crores and employment of 67.5 thousand persons. The number of small scale industries has also increased from 9,119 in 1979-80 to 33,820 till 1988-89. The total capital investment of these industries till the year 1988-89 stood at Rs. 38,570.63 lakh and employment in the small scale sector was 2.5 lakh persons.[5]

However, the industrial progress of the state is not very much encouraging. In 1986-87 per capita gross output in industry was Rs. 788.4 in the state, whereas it was Rs. 1,713.2 at the all India level. Again in the year referred above, the per capita value added by manufacture was much low with Rs. 142.7 in the state as against the national level of Rs. 329.1.

It is on account of all these factors, that greater emphasis is put on for the development of village and cottage industries in the state. The is considered more desirable on account of the fact that they are low cost units, use mainly local resources and promise a higher production and employment in the rural sector. It is seen from available data that the number of artisan units have increased from 31.5 thousand in the year 1979-80 to 1.10 lakhs units in 1988-89. The capital investment and number of persons employed have also increased from Rs. 529.4 lakhs to Rs. 2,726.7 lakhs and 59.3 thousand persons to 1.9 lakh persons respectively in the year under reference.

Trade and Commerce

The composition of trade in Orissa mostly includes merchandise goods like rice, fruits, vegetables and jute etc. In the external trade sector the main items of exports are fish and fish products, mineral products, cloth and textiles etc. In the year 1988-89 the percentage share of export of metallurgical products, mineral products and handlooms to the total exports was 66.0, 23.2, 6.1 and 3.1 per cent respectively.[6] It is however noticed that the percentage share of trade and commerce in the total income of the state is not encouraging. Since there has taken place a growing preference for artisan based products in the recent years, the scope for the expansion of trade and commerce need be given utmost importance.

Infrastructure

The infrastructure development; though has increased considerably in the state, yet it still appears to be inadequate. In relation to average road length per lakh of population, the state's figure compares shyly to that of national average. Furthermore, number of buses per 1000 sq. km. of area in the state whereas stood at 16 in the year 1987-88, the same was 78 at the all-India level. Railway root length per 1000 sq.km. of area was only 12.7 kms in the state whereas it was 19.9 kms. at the all-India level in 1988-89. Furthermore, the infrastructural development is practically poor in the rural areas. Connection between one village to the other is very often affected, due to non-availability of good roads.

Resource Potentials

As against these problems, the state is however, endowed with abundant natural resources. These natural resources often provide scope for the development of different types of industries in the state.

1. Forest Resources

The total area covered under forests in the state was 57.2 thousand sq. kms. in the year 1989-90. In terms of percentage, in the year 1989-90, the proportion of forest area to the total geographical area was 36 per cent. In the year 1989-90, the percentage share of revenue collected from major forest products to that of total revenue collected from the forest constitutes 81.0 per cent, while it is only 6.5 per cent in case of minor forest products. However, the minor products provide opportunities for the establishment of forest based artisan units like that of hand-made paper, manufacture of gum and rasin, sheelac, cottage match, fire works and etc.

2. Mineral Resources

The total mineral resources of the state in percentage

terms account for about 15.6 per cent of the total mineral reserves of the country. Orissa is a leading source of chromite, bauxite, coal, iron ore, nickel, fire clay, dolomite, and vanadium ore, which constitute upto 97.0, 57.5, 21.5, 17.8, 64.8, 12.0, 10.9 and 10.8 per cents respectively to the total mineral deposits of the country. They may lead to the establishment of some mineral based artisan industrial units like pottery units, lime products units, stone carving, slate making and pencil making units etc.

3. *Marine Resources*

Orissa as a maritime state offers a wide scope for the utilisation and exploration of marine resources. The entire coast line of 480 kms. provides ample opportunities for the exploration of marine products. They can very well help for the growth of some artisan units like that of lime product units, sea shell and crunch units, and fish processing units etc.

3. *Land Resources*

The industrial units like that of processing of pulses and cereals, palmgur and palm products making units, gur and khandasari, units producing ghani oil and etc. can be developed with agriculture as the primary source.

5. *Power*

By the end of March 1989, 29.2 thousand villages of the state have been electrified, which accounts for 62.1 per cent of total number of villages in the state.[7] With the supply of adequate power the artisans will be in a position to use modern tools and equipments, and improved technology in their units.

Institutional Financing

Lack of finance is the crucial problem faced by the artisans. In the past they depended upon unorganised institutions for their requirements of capital, which was more costly and was not meeting the full requirements of the artisans. In course of time a wide spectrum of institutional financing agencies have come into existence in the state to meet the requirements of the rural artisans. These institutional agencies are Cooperative Banks, Commercial Banks, Regional Rural Banks and Orissa State Financial Corporation.

Development of Artisan Based Units

Orissa has a rich tradition of having a large number of village and cottage industries. The artisan units like; stone carving of Konark and Puri, applique works of Pipil, filigree works of Cuttack, Sabai Grass works of Mayurbhanj, and horn works of Ganjam etc. have always attracted the attention of the people of the country and the outside. The state, apart from the few mentioned above, has a large number of artisan based units of diversified types, spread over in different parts of the state. However, these units are mainly classified into five categories viz., Khadi and Village Industries, Handlooms, Sericulture, Handicrafts and Coir Industries.

Needs and Requirements of Rural Artisans

It is against this background that an attempt is made to analyse the needs and aspirations of rural artisans.

(i) *Establishment*: Artisan units are mostly carried out on household basis. Rarely they go for hired premises for the operation of their units. In the first place, hired premises are rarely available in the rural areas. Secondly, wherever they are available the rents are exorbitant, which the artisans find it difficult to meet.

(ii) *Products*: Mainly the articles produced by the rural artisans include articles of common use such as bamboo and cane furniture, hand woven clothes, pottery and door and table mats etc. The second category consists of products having aesthetic values. These articles are patta paintings, applique works, dokra castings and filigree works etc.

(iii) *Raw Materials*: Rural artisans mostly procure the raw materials locally. At times raw materials are supplied by the Co-operative Societies to the artisans. However scarcity and irregular supply of raw materials is the most important problem faced by rural artisans.

(iv) *Marketing*: Marketing of artisan's products is essential. In the absence of marketing, whatever products the artisans would produce may not fetch a remunerative price. Absence of transport and communication facilities and absence of any organised institutions to shoulder the responsibility of the marketing of the products to a great extent affects the sale of products. As a result of this the artisans very often fall prey to the hands of middle men.

(v) *Storage*: Artisans in normal situations do not prefer to store articles. However, at times when demand for the product is slack, they prefer storage of articles for future sale. But due to want of finance and space they find it difficult to store the articles. Particularly, stone carving units, pottery units, basket making units etc. require large storing spaces which the artisans find it difficult to provide. Artisans working under organised units however, are comfortably placed in this regard.

(vi) *Finance*: Finance is the most important requirement of the rural artisans. According to all-India Debt investment Survey, 1971, 39 per cent of the rural artisans were in debt. While debt asset ratio formed 42 per cent, the institutional credit amounted to only 4.8 and 7.4 per cent to the total debt raised by the artisans in the country and in the state respectively[8]. However the situation has undergone a change in recent years.

(vii) *Technology*: Rural artisans operate with simple technology. They use simple machines and tools. These are mostly outdated and obsolete. In order to improve their competitiveness, technological upgradation may be encouraged.

Looking at these needs and requirements of rural artisans in the state, it is of utmost necessity that proper attention be paid for fulfilling these requirements. It is against this background that it becomes necessary to make an in-depth study about the socio-economic background of Puri district where the sample study has been undertaken.

PURI DISTRICT

Puri district, the land of temples and monuments bears a testimony of great traditional antiquity in the field of art and architecture since the time immemorial. The district is also acclaimed for having a large network of village and cottage industries producing artistic products of aesthetic value. However the inflow of machine made products competing severely with the products of village and cottage industries have contributed for the decline of later type of industries. Besides the patronage and assistance which was previously rendered by kings and emperors to the artisans was not available on account of their decline. Inspite of this, that the village and cottage industries have continued to stay in the field is of creditable performance. Although the district has a number of traditional units, yet in the recent years a number of non-traditional units have come into existence.

The preference for Puri district amongst other districts arises from the fact that, most of the categories of village and cottage industries which are found at the state level are seen in the district. Broadly the village and cottage industries are classified mainly into five categories, such as Khadi and Village Industries, Handlooms, Sericulture, Handicrafts, and Coir. Of all these categories visible at the state level, Puri district has almost all the types of industries except Sericulture. Of the total number of Khadi and Village Industries numbering 26 as listed by KVIC as on 1988, a bulk of these industries are located in the rural areas of the district. The district is favoured by having Khadi and Village Industries Board (KVIB) which work as the regional office of KVIC. Handloom is another important artisan sector, which is being practised by most of the artisans living in the rural areas of the district. Puri is also the headquarter of the organisations like Orissa Handloom Development Corporations and Orissa State Handloom Weavers Co-operative Society Ltd. Sericulture artisan units are mostly located in the hilly and tribal areas of the state and they are mostly not found in adequate number in the district under consideration. The district has also a total number of 28 types of handicraft units, out of 50 types of handicraft units located at the state level. Furthermore, out of the total number of 35 thousand handicraft artisans engaged in various craft, the district is having nearly 12 thousand handicraft artisans. On account of large scale coconut production a number of coir product units have also come into existence in the district.[9]

Socio-economic Feature of Puri District

Puri, one of the coastal districts of the state, is not only famous for its great tradition of art and craft but also for its other historic antiquities and religious sanctuaries. Its unique and historical monuments like the Jagannath temple at Puri, the Lingaraj temple at Bhubaneswar and the Sun Temple at Konark are famous in the world.

Population

There has taken place a significant growth of population between 1971 and 1981. The percentage rate of growth of population between this period stood at 25 per cent. It is observed that the density of population in Puri district whereas stood at 230 per square km in the year 1971, the same increased to 287 sq.km. in 1981. The density of population in 1981 in the state, however, stood at 169 persons. Available data reveal that the district has 24.88 lakhs of rural population and 4.32 lakhs of urban population according to 1981 census. It is evident that nearly 85 per cent of the total population of the district is concentrated alone in the rural areas. It is further revealed that the proportion of Scheduled Castes and Scheduled Tribes population to the total population of the district is 16.4 per cent. The district has a total number of 14.7 lakhs of male and 14.3 lakhs of female population. Out of the total population of the district they account for 51.0 per cent and 49.0 per cent respectively. Available data show that 13.3 lakhs of population living in the district are literates. The rate of literacy in the district is calculated to be 45.5 per cent. The rate of literacy among the persons living in urban areas was much greater with 63.5 per cent, while that of 42.4 per cent for the rural areas. Only 8.1 lakh of population are the main workers. The percentage share of main workers to that of total population is of 29.1 per cent. It indicates that nearly two thirds of the total population are not working while one third of the total population is engaged in various occupational activities. It is noticed that a majority of population or nearly 67.6 per cent is engaged in agricultural activities. As against this the proportion of workers engaged in household activities and tertiary activities accounted for 3.4 per cent and 29.1 per cent in the year 1981 respectively.[10]

Agriculture

Agriculture is the principal occupation of the district. Majority of the total population are engaged in agriculture for their livelihood and occupation. The total gross cropped area in the district in 1988-89 is 746 thousand hectares. Of the total geographical area this accounts for nearby 70 per cent. And the net area sown to gross cropped area is 62.3 per cent in the year 1988-89. It is further revealed that irrigated area accounts for 53 per cent, of the total net sown area in the district in the year 1988-89. Cropping patterns of the district shows lopsided development. The available data reveal that nearly 77.8 per cent of gross cropped area are covered by food crops. As against this area covered by non-food crops account for only 22.2 per cent of the total gross cropped area in 1988-89. This is an indication of this fact that diversification of agriculture has not taken place in a rapid stride.[11]

The performance of agriculture in the district is however, beset with various problems. Percentage of irrigated area to total gross cropped area is 32.8 per cent accounting for a low proportion. It is also noticed that a bulk of the land holdings in the district belong to the category of small and marginal holdings. In the year 1985-86, the marginal and small holding stood at 86.8 per cent but they accounted for only 55.2 per cent of the total area operated. This indicates that there is preponderance of marginal and small farmers in the district, but the area operated by these farmers accounts for a low proportion. Since these farmers are unable to be absorbed in agriculture round the year, for various problems, it is necessary to engage them in viable employment activities outside the farm sector.[12]

It is further seen that the agriculture has not gathered adequate momentum in the district. It continues to be traditional and non-commercial. It is seen from the fact that the proportion of area covered by high yielding varieties of paddy is 23.9 per cent of the total gross cropped area. Even the consumption of fertilizer per hectare which is 26.6 kg has continued to be low compared to the state average. Even, mechanisation of agriculture has not penetrated deep into the agricultural sector. As most of the land holdings are very small in size, use of various modern farm machinery is becoming difficult. At the end of 1988 there were only 171 tractors in the district. Credit which constitutes an essential input for agricultural development is also inadequate and not timely available. All these above factors contribute significantly for the low productivity and slow growth of agriculture.

Poverty, Underemployment and Unemployment

Agriculture provides employment to a large section of the population in the district. But as a seasonal occupation, it does not provide employment for most part of the year. Due to lower productivity in the agricultural sector, accompanied with continuous growth in labour force, the unemployment and underemployment situation is becoming more aggravated in recent years. Moreover, underemployment and unemployment situation in the district as a whole pose a great danger to the economy of the district. According to the available data the employment seekers including both educated and uneducated persons in the district has increased from 1.4 lakhs to 1.74 lakh persons, during the period 1981 to 1987. It is noticed that a bulk of the population living in the rural areas of the district are poor. Absence of work in the rural areas and inability of agriculture to absorb all the population round the year in gainful employment activities, to a great extent contribute for the poverty of the people.[13]

Profile of Artisan-based Units

In the industrial field, the district does not have any large scale industries. However, there is larger concentration of medium, small scale and artisan based units in the district. The profile of the artisan based units taken from the field study are discussed below:

(i) *Pottery*: The art of pottery making is as old as the trade itself. The clay products in different forms were in use since very ancient times. It is estimated that about 11.2 lakhs persons are engaged in pottery activities in the country. Available data show that the share of S.C. and S.T. artisans to the total overall employment in pottery industry is upto 25 per cent and share of female artisans to that of total employment is upto 30 per cent.[14] At present the major states contributing to the overall performance of pottery are Maharashtra, Uttar Pradesh, Haryana, Andhra Pradesh, Kerala, Rajasthan, Gujarat and Tamil Nadu.

Pottery as a major village and cottage industry is developed throughout the state of Orissa, and the district. Artisans are mostly found in each and every village. As a labour intensive trade it employs the whole family of the artisan. The trade being seasonal in nature does not provide employment throughout the year. Key problems relating to the pottery units are; lack of adequate availability of fuel, such as cow dung cake, coal ash and slack coal.

(ii) *Bamboo Works*: Besides Orissa, the cane and bamboo craft is also seen in states like Jammu & Kashmir, Maharastra, Kerala, Punjab, Assam and Tamil Nadu. The industry was included under the list of village industries of KVIC since 1968-69. Bamboo works units are also being developed in the state and in the districts like Cuttack, Ganjam, Sambalpur, Puri and Koraput. But maximum number of families engaged in cane and bamboo works are seen in Puri district. Out of 3389 families engaged in the trade, 551 families were living in Puri district. Again in Puri district they are concentrated in places like Banapur, Ranapur, Chandanpur, Bhubaneswar, Narendrapur, Khurda, Balanga and etc.[15] A large section of population particularly from the weaker sections are engaged in the production of various household articles such as baskets, ladders, mats etc. The bamboo works require simple techniques, which is very much labour intensive. The bamboo work artisan units face severe competition from the plastic industry. Again the raw materials like bamboo is not available easily in recent times due to deforestation and other alternative uses of it.

(iii) *Handloom*: The Handloom, one of the important artisan units is seen mostly in each and every village of the state as well as in the district. However, handloom weavers are mostly concentrated in the districts like Sambalpur, Bolangir, Ganjam, Cuttack, Puri and etc. It is estimated that as on 1988, out of the total 81,119 number of looms covered under Co-operative sector in the state, 14 thousand looms are located only in the district of Puri. Again of the total production of clothes of 432.86 lakh square metres in the year 1988 in organised sector of the state, 120.87 lakhs square metres of cloth are produced in the district. It reveals that most of the weaver artisans in the district work under co-operatives.[16]

(iv) *Brass and Bell Metal*: The largest concentration of handicraft artisans in the district is in Brass and Bell metal craft. The craft is also practised in each and every district of the state, but it is mostly concentrated in the district like Ganjam, Puri, Cuttack and Sambalpur. In relation to number of families engaged in this trade, Puri occupies the second place, the first place being occupied by Ganjam. Again in the district of Puri these artisans are mostly seen in places like, Balakati, Bainchua, Kantilo and Itamati. Of the total number of 17,950 families engaged in this trade in the state, 4,250 families are living in Puri District. In terms of percentage, it stood at 23.7 per cent to the total families engaged in the state. The craft is labour intensive in nature. The artisans mostly live in clusters and the craft is mostly carried out by a particular caste called 'Kansari' or Iron smith, on hereditary basis.

(v) *Stone Carving*: Stone carving is one of the most popular craft of the state and also of the district. The craft is mostly seen in the districts like Puri and Cuttack. Of the total 687 stone carving artisan families, 466 families or 67.8 per cent of families were there in Puri district. Again in Puri, the craft is mostly located in places like Puri, Bhubaneswar, Konark, Tapanga, Odagaon and Jagamara and etc. The craftsmen are mostly progenies of the artisans who built the world famous Sun Temple at Konark, Jagannath Temple at Puri, and Lingaraj Temple at Bhubaneswar. The products have got good demand inside and outside of the country. The craft required skilled craftsmanship, artistic skill and simple traditional techniques. Though the craft was spread in so many places yet there existed only one Cooperative Society for Stone carving at 'Pathuria Sahi' in Puri.

(vi) *Applique Work*: The other important handicraft item of the district is applique craft. The applique items are mostly decorative and colourful. They depict a harmonious combination of both cloth and motifs. The products generally include garden umbrellas, canopies, letter bags, shoulder bags, table mats, ladies bags, wall hangings and etc. The craftsmen engaged in the trade are mostly seen in the districts like Ganjam, Phulbani and Puri. Out of the total 625 applique artisan families living in the state, 540 artisan families are there in Puri district, which constitute upto 72.0 per cent to the total. Apart from Pipli, this craftsmen are also seen in places like Balanga, Banamalipur, Sakhigopal, Puri and etc.[17] Applique work as a household activity was carried on a hereditary basis, by a particular caste called Darji. But at present the craft is being undertaken by artisans belonging to other caste also. The craft is very labour intensive in nature and it provides employment to the entire family of the artisan.[18] Of all the types of applique items, garden umbrella is found to be more remunerative to the artisans. It has good demand in foreign countries.

(vii) ***Patta Chitra*:** Patta Chitra a typical Orissan painting, originated from a village called Raghurajpur of district Puri has acquired worldwide reputation, being prominently sought for in the export market. Besides Puri, Patta Chitra artisans are also mostly seen in the district like Ganjam. However, they are concentrated in Puri district to a greater extent. Out of the 406 Patta Chitra artisan families living in the state as a whole, 350 families were located in various places of the Puri district, like Raghurajpur, Puri and Bhubaneswar etc. In percentage term, it stood at 86.0 per cent to the total families seen in Orissa. Due to larger concentration of Patta Chitra and other types of artisans in Raghurajpur, the village has been termed as the craft village, in the state as well as at the national level. The artisans mostly produce paintings of human and animal figures basing upon historical and mythological backgrounds. This craft mostly originated from the Patta Chitras made on the various walls of Jagannath Temple, Puri. While making the Patta Chitra, the artisans mostly use traditional vegetable colour and use some simple painting materials. Due to high cost Patta Chitra products are generally purchased by the affluent society, in the community.

(viii) *Papier Mache*: Another handicraft item which is much in demand at present is the craft of Papier Mache. The craft constitute making of paper masks of various Gods and Goddesses worshipped in the state and masks of various animals and birds. Only in the district of Puri, 105 Papier Machie artisan families are located in various places, like Bhubaneswar, Puri and Raghurajpur, etc. The craft items requires simple labour as a result of which mostly women artisans are seen to be engaged in this craft.

(ix) *Beads Making*: Artisans engaged in the trade prepare garlands out of a particular type of locally seeds of a nut, produced from cane plant. It is rare agro-based village craft being practised in the district. At certain places it is seen that all the inhabitants living in a particular village, are engaged in the craft. The artisans mostly belong to Scheduled Caste Community. The craft is so simple that it employs male, female and even the children members of the family. The product is very cheap, and are sold at places of pilgrimage, like Mathura, Brindaban, Varanasi and etc. The craft is very much rewarding but due to shortage of raw materials lack of finance and storage facility the artisans face a serious problem while performing their trade.

(x) *Coir Works*: Coir industry bears a vast potential for development in the district . Due to concentration of coconut production a large number of artisans both in private and co-operative sector are manufacturing different coir goods. Sakhigopal area in Puri district is identified as a growth centre of coir product. A coir training centre and a coconut plantation research institute are located at Sakhigopal. The area accounts for 43.66 per cent of the total area under coconut plantation in Orissa and for 55.71 per cent of the total output at the state level.[19]

Socio-Economic Profile of Sample Artisans

Socio-economic profile of the sample artisans in relation to their premises and establishment, nature of organisation, caste, education, skill, training and etc. are discussed below:

(i) Premises and Establishments

The most important nature of artisan units is that they are carried out in household basis. The main industrial activity as well as marketing is also performed mostly at the door step of the artisans. It is revealed from the sample study undertaken, that the most of the artisans have inherited their skills as well as their workshop and industrial establishment from the family. Empirical data shows that out of total 120 artisans studied, 116 artisans had their own industrial establishment, while rest of the artisans numbering four were undertaking their industrial activities in hired industrial establishments, belonging to some relatives. This is seen from Table 3.6.

Table 3.6

Ownership of Industrial Establishment

	No. of Artisans				*Total*	
Ownership of work establishment	*Male*	*% to the total*	*Female*	*% to the total*	*Nos.*	*% to the total*
Type of Ownership						
(i) Owned Premises	95	95.9	21	100.0	116	97.0
(ii) Hired Premises	4	4.1	–	–	4	3.0
Total (i + ii)	99	100.0	21	100.0	120	100.0

Source : Data compiled from field study, 1989.

It was revealed that, the importance of industrial establishment or premise was mostly nil in case of most of the artisan units studied. However it is required to a greater extent in case of artisan units like handloom, stone carving, bell metal works, applique and pottery.

(ii) Nature of Organisation

The nature of artisan units is such that they are principally managed by the artisan himself, single handedly. The study shows that they were working also, under co-operative societies in an organised manner. Empirical study shows that the artisan units like bell metal craft, pottery works and weaving numbering 62 were functioning under their respective co-operative societies. While all others numbering 58 were working as single proprietorship. In percentage term the proportion of artisans working under co-operative to that of total sample artisans studied constitute up to 51.7 per cent, while it was upto 48.3 per cent in case of artisans performing their trade individually*.

(iii) Caste

Caste affiliation among various artisans and their trade is very much significant. In general the artisans mostly have adopted the trade, not as an economic choice but are engaged in the occupation, by birth.

Table 3.7

Distribution of Sample Artisans as Per Their Skill Inherited/Learned

Skill acquired	*Male*		*Female*		*Total*	
	No.	*% to the total*	*No.*	*% to the total*	*No.*	*% to the total*
A. Inherited	99	100.0	9	47.3	108	90.0
B. Learned						
(i) OSHC	–	–	12	52.7	12	10.0
Total (A+B)	99	100.0	21	100.0	120	100.0

Source : Data compiled from field study, 1989.

* Data based on field study.

Empirical data exhibited in Table 3.7 show that only 12 artisans who are engaged in trades like coir and papier machie had learned the trade through a training programme and have not inherited the occupation by birth. In percentage term the proportion of artisans who were in the trade, by caste or by birth, to the total artisans studied, constitute upto 90 per cent while it was up to only 10 per cent, in case of artisans who had learned the trade. At present in the trades like applique, patta chitra and stone carving etc., some new entrants from other social groups are also making headway to enter, as the trades are becoming more attractive and rewarding.

(iv) Male, Female Participation, Earner and Dependent Ratio

Sex-wise classification of sample artisans shows that out of 120 sample units studied the number of total female artisans constitute 21 in number, whereas it is 99 in case of male artisans. The proportion of female and male artisans to the total sample artisans, in percentage term constitute upto 17.5 per cent and 82.5 per cent respectively. This is shown in Table 3.8.

It was revealed that participation rate of women artisans was very significant in trades like coir and papier machie, as all the artisans engaged in these trade numbering 12 were women. As against this, all the artisan studied under the category like bell metal, applique, patta chitra and stone carving numbering 45 were performed by only male artisans. Other artisan units coming under the category called weaving, beads making, bamboo basket making and pottery were being owned by both male as well as female artisans. However, it was noticed that due to nature of labour intensiveness, almost all the sample artisan units studied had to depend upon women members of the family either partly of fully to carry out the trade. It is noticed that the trades like coir, papier machie, applique works and others may very well be performed by women artisans.

Table 3.8

Sex-wise Composition of the Sample Artisans

Sl. No.	*Artisan Units*	*Male*		*Female*		*Total*	
		No.	*% to the total*	*No.*	*% to the total*	*No.*	*% to the total*
1.	Pottery	12	70.0	5	30.0	17	(100.0)
2.	Bamboo Works	8	88.0	1	12.0	9	(100.0)
3.	Weaving	27	92.0	2	8.0	27	(100.0)
4.	Brass and bell metal works	25	100.0	–	–	25	(100.0)
5.	Stone Carving	4	100.0	–	–	4	(100.0)
6.	Applique	12	100.0	–	–	12	(100.0)
7.	Patta Chitra	4	100.0	–	–	4	(100.0)
8.	Papier Mache	–	–	6	100.0	6	(100.0)
9.	Beads Making	9	90.0	1	10.0	10	(100.0)
10.	Coir Works	–	–	6	100.0	6	(100.0)
	Total	99	82.5	21	17.5	120	(100.0)

Source: Data complied from the field study, 1989.

A further classification of sample artisans shows that majority of them were earners or were earning for their family. some artisans engaged in the trades like applique, and patta chitra, belonging to age group of 66 years and above were also seen to be engaged in the trade as an earner artisan. Empirical data as shown in Table 3.9 reveals that out of total sample artisan units studied most of the artisans numbering 118 are working as earners, while only two artisans engaged in the trades like bell metal craft were found to depend upon family for their bread and butter to some extent and can be termed as dependant. As revealed by the artisans themselves, the bell metal work which requires heavy physical labour was mainly responsible for

Table 3.9

Age and Sex Composition of the Sample Artisans According to Their Economic Status, 1989

Age Group	Male Earner		Female Earner		Total Earner		Dependant		Total Earner plus dependant
	No.	% to the total	No.	% to the total	No.	% to the total	Male	Female	
18 – 25	14	14.4	3	14.3	17	14.4	–	–	17
26 – 35	28	28.8	9	42.8	37	31.4	–	–	37
36 – 45	27	27.8	5	23.8	32	27.1	–	–	32
46 – 55	22	22.6	3	14.3	25	21.2	2	–	27
56 – 65	3	3.11	–	–	3	2.5	–	–	3
66 - & above	3	3.11	1	4.8	4	3.4	–	–	4
Total	97	100.0	21	100.0	118 (98.3%)	100.0	2 (1.7%)	–	120 (100)

Source: Data compiled from field study, 1989
Figures in parentheses indicate percentage to the total.

their physical disability and quick approach of old age and made them to depend on the family.

(v) Educational Status

Educational status of the sample artisans shows that among the sample artisans 61 persons were found to be literates and 59 persons were found to be illiterates. Empirical study exhibited in Table 3.10 shows that illiteracy among the artisans is quite great. 49.0 per cent of the artisans studied were illiterates in the sense that they did not know ever simple alphabets. Of the total number of illiterates, 75 per cent were men and 25 per cent were the women. Again out of the total artisans coming under literates, 90 per cent constitute males whereas 10 per cent constitute females.

Table 3.10

Educational Status of the Sample Artisans: 1989

Sl. No.	*Level of Education*	*Male*		*Female*		*Total*	
		No.	*% to the total*	*No.*	*% to the total*	*No.*	*% to the total*
1.	Illiterate	44 (75.0)	44.4	15 (25.0)	71.5	59 (100.0)	49.1
2.	Literate						
	(a) Below Primary	27	27.8	5	23.8	32	26.6
	(b) Below Secondary	22	22.6	1	4.76	23	19.1
	(c) Secondary	3	3.1	–	–	3	2.5
	(d) Intermediate	1	1.0	–	–	1	0.8
	(e) Graduate	2	2.0	–	–	2	1.6
	Total (a+b+c+d+e)	55 90.0)	55.5	6 (10.0)	28.6	61 (100.0)	50.8
	Grand Total (1+2)	99	100.0	21	100.0	120	100.0

Source : Data compiled from the field study, 1989.
Figures in parentheses indicate per cent to the total.

It was also found that of the total literate artisans, nearly 26.6 per cent had received education below primary level and nearly 19.1 per cent have received education below secondary stage. It was observed that illiteracy among women artisans was greater in relation to that of men. Of the total female artisans, 71 per cent were illiterate and 24 per cent were having education only below primary level.

(vi) Skill, Training and Entrepreneurship

Distribution of sample artisans as per their skills showed that our of the total sample artisans 108 sample artisans have inherited their skill from their forefathers. While the remaining artisans numbering 12, who were mostly engaged in crafts like coir and papier machie, have acquired the skill through training programmes initiated by State Handicraft Corporation. This was exhibited in an earlier Table 3.7.

Besides these 12, there were 18 other sample artisans who had received training for improving their previous traditional skill. So sample artisans numbering 30 or 25 per cent of total artisans had received training for improvement of their original skill. Artisans engaged in units like weaving, bell metal and etc. have received this type of training. So it is a fact that the number of artisans receiving training is very less. On the otherhand, artisans who failed to receive training account for 90. Percentagewise, they form 75 per cent of the total artisans. This is shown in Table 3.11.

With lack of literacy and lack of sufficient training facility it is very much imperative to state that the artisans have limited entrepreneurial skill and initiative. Due to limited knowledge they even utilise the unskilled and degraded technology and tools which are obsolete. They are also mostly unorganised in their trade. And at times when they form any organisation, lack of knowledge debarred them from managing the organisation properly.

Table 3.11

Craftwise Distribution of Sample Artisans of Training Received

Sl. No.	*Type of Artisans*	*No. of sample artisans*		*No. of artisans received training*		*No. of artisans not received training*	
1.	Pottery	17	(100.0)	5	(29.0)	12	(0.71)
2.	Bamboo Works	9	(100.0)		–	9	(100.0)
3.	Weaving	27	(100.0)	9	(33.0)	18	(67.0)
4.	Bell metal	25	(100.0)	2	(8.0)	23	(91.0)
5.	Stone Carving	4	(100.0)		–	4	(100.0)
6.	Applique	12	(100.0)		–	12	(100.0)
7.	Patta Chitra	4	(100.0)	2	(50.0)	2	(50.0)
8.	Papier Machie	6	(100.0)	6	(100.0)		–
9.	Beads Making	10	(100.0)		–	10	(100.0)
10.	Coir Works	6	(100.0)	6	(100.0)		–
Total		120	(100.0)	30	(25.0)	90	(75.0)

Source: Data compiled from field study, 1989.
N.B. Figures in parentheses indicate percentage to the total.

(vii) Nature of Products

Rural artisans studied mostly produce two types of articles. Firstly the goods which possess general utility are the pottery items, bamboo baskets, cheap towels, dhotis, bag, door mat, and etc. Secondly, the artisans also produce goods of decorative value, which cost more and are generally purchased by the affluent groups and also command a good export market. The stone carving, applique and Patta Chitra products are coming under the second category. It is noticed that artisans were producing mostly the traditional items. Due to lack of knowledge and sufficient training in this matter they were unable to inject new ideas and innovative thinking into the trade. But to attract more customers and market, new items may be introduced. But simultaneously the traditional nature of the craft will have to be maintained in the craft like applique, patta chitra and stone carving.

(viii) Nature of Employment

Most of the artisans studied were working as owned artisans and were thus self-employed. Out of total artisans studied nearly 98.4 per cent were self employed, whereas the 1.6 per cent were working for others as hired artisan. This is shown in Table 3.12.

Table 3.12

Distribution of Sample Artisans by Nature of Work

Sl. No.	*Nature of Work*	*No. of artisan*		*Total*	
		Male	*Female*	*No.*	*% to the total*
1.	Owned Artisans	97 (98.0)	21 (100.0)	118	98.4
2.	Hired Artisans	2 (2.0)	–	2	1.6
	Total	99 (100.00)	21 (100.0)	120	100.0

Source : Data complied from Field Study, 1985.
Figures in parentheses indicate percentage to the total.

It was observed from Table 3.13 that artisans had mostly accepted their trade as their principal occupation. But as most of the artisan activities are seasonal in nature, the artisans at times have to depend upon some other secondary sources. It was noticed that artisan units like pottery, handicrafts and etc. generally suffer a lot in the rainy season. So at times, the artisans made themselves engaged in agricultural land as farmers or as agricultural labourers. The Table 2.13 shows that of the total sample artisans studied 21.7 per cent were having other subsidiary occupations, whereas 78.3 per cent of artisans studied had no subsidiary occupations, other than the artisan works. This can be seen from Table 3.13.

Table 3.13

Occupational Pattern of Sample Artisans: Principal vrs. Subsidiary

Sl. No.	*Occupational Category*	*Total No. of sample artisans*		*Artisans having no subsidiary occupation*		*Artisans having any subsidiary occupation*	
1.	Pottery	17	(100.0)	12	(70.6)	5	(29.4)
2.	Bamboo Works	9	(100.0)	4	(44.0)	5	(56.0)
3.	Weaving	27	(100.0)	19	(70.4)	8	(29.6)
4.	Ball Metal	25	(100.0)	21	(84.0)	4	(16.0)
5.	Stone Carving	4	(100.0)	4	(100.0)	–	
6.	Applique	12	(100.0)	12	(100.0)	–	
7.	Patta Chitra	4	(100.0)	4	(100.0)	–	
8.	Papier Machie	6	(100.0)	6	(100.0)	–	
9.	Beads Making	10	(100.0)	6	(60.0)	4	(40.0)
10.	Coir Works	6	(100.0)	6	(100.0)	–	
	Total :	120	(100.0)	94	(78.3)	26	(21.7)

Source : Data compiled from field study, 1989.
Figures in parentheses indicated percentage to the total.

(ix) Resources

Except some particular type of rural industrial activities most of the types of artisan units depend on available local resources. At times artisan clusters are developed at place, where resources required for the unit is plentily available. As for example coir products units of Sakhigopal area are mainly developed only due to massive coconut production in that area. Other trades like pottery and bamboo basket makings and etc. are also developed at places where they get plenty of resources.

(x) Raw Material used

Rural artisans mostly use locally available raw materials. However due to financial inadequacy, the artisans are not in a position to take full advantage of buying total requirement of raw materials. So at times they were forced, to buy from local merchants or traders at a high price, which is not always possible. At times they are forced to borrow raw materials from traders and repay the loan in terms of finished product, for which they do not get the required price. Artisans working under co-operatives also face problems, due to irregular supply of raw materials.

Table 3.14

Distribution of Sample Artisans of Sources of Collection of Raw Materials

Sl. No.	*Artisan Units*	*No. of sample artisans*		*Collecting raw materials from Co-Soc.*		*Collecting raw materials by own effort*	
1.	Pottery	17	(100.0)		–	17	(100.0)
2.	Bamboo Works	9	(100.0)		–	9	(100.0)
3.	Weaving	27	(100.0)	27	(100.0)	–	
4.	Ball Metal	25	(100.0)	25	(100.0)	–	
5.	Stone Carving	4	(100.0)		–	4	(100.0)
6.	Applique	12	(100.0)		–	12	(100.0)
7.	Patta Chitra	4	(100.0)		–	4	(100.0)
8.	Papier Mache	6	(100.0)		–	6	(100.0)
9.	Beads Making	10	(100.0)		–	10	(100.0)
10.	Coir Works	6	(100.0)		–	6	(100.0)
Total		120	(100.0)	52	(43.0)	68	(57.0)

Source: Data compiled from the Field Study, 1989.
Figures in parentheses indicate percentage to the total.

Table 3.14 shows that of the total units units studied, nearyly 43 per cent of the artisan units were, having raw materials from their co-operatives. Bell metal and weving artisans were included in the category. While the remaining units constituting 57 per cent. had to make their own arrangement of raw materials.

(xi) Technology

In the field study it was noticed that almost all the artisan units studied had adopted labour intensive technology. They mostly use ageold traditional tools and equipments. There is necessity of introducing better technology of such type that it will not disturb the traditionality, and number of labour employed, but side by side will be more productive.

(xii) Incentives and Subsidies

For the growth and development of artisan sector, the sector has been variously encouraged by state as well as central level organisations like Small Industries Development Organisation (SIDO), Khadi and Village Industries Commission and Boards (KVIC and KVIBs), Coir Board, Development Commissioner for Handlooms, Development Commissioner for Handicraft, Central Silk Board and etc. Besides an extensive co-operative organisation in the state and district provide marketing support to handloom products. The State Emporias, Central Cottage Industries Emporium, Khadi and Gramodyog Bhawans/ Bhandars, Coir Board Showroom, State Handicraft Corporation and Handloom Corporation and etc. are some of the organisations, which supply incentives to the artisans through marketing. Government at times give incentives to the artisans through reduction and even exemption of octroi charges on transportation of artisan products. Rebate is also allowed for better marketing.

Institutional financing agencies provide the most important incentive to the rural artisans through financial assistance with a subsidy component. Out of the total 120 sample artisans, artisans numbering 37 had availed loan with a subsidy component. This is seen from Table 3.15. Those artisans who were financed under the schemes like IRDP, SC or ST and KVIC category have availed subsidy of 33.3 per cent, 25 per cent and 44 per cent respectively. Table 3.16 shows disbursement of subsidy to the various sample artisans loanees as per different schemes.

Table 3.15

Distribution of Sample Artisans Received Loan with and Without Subsidy

Sl. No.	*Name of the Artisans Units*	*No. of Artisans received loan with a subsidy component*		*No. of artisans received without subsidy component*		*Total No. of Artisan loanees studied*	
1.	Pottery	17	(100.0)	–	–	17	(100.0)
2.	Bamboo Works	4	(44.0)	5	(56.0)	9	(100.0)
3.	Weaving	–	–	27	(100.0)	27	(100.0)
4.	Ball Metal	–	–	25	(100.0)	25	(100.0)
5.	Stone Carving	–	–	4	(100.0)	4	(100.0)
6.	Applique	–	–	12	(100.0)	12	(100.0)
7.	Patta Chitra	–	–	4	(100.0)	4	(100.0)
8.	Papier Machie	6	(100.0)	–	-	6	(100.0)
9.	Beads Making	4	(40.0)	6	(60.0)	10	(100.0)
10.	Coir Works	6	(100.0)	–	–	6	(100.0)
	Total :	37	(31.0)	83	(69.0)	120	(100.0)

Source : Data compiled from the Field Study, 1989.
Figures in parentheses indicate percentage to the total.

Table 3.16

Distribution of Sample Artisans Received Loan Under Different Development Programmes

(in Rs.)

	Types of Schemes	*No. of artisans financed under development schemes*	*Amount of loan sanctioned*	*No. of artisans availing subsidy*	*Amount of subsidy disbursed*	*% of subsidy to loan*
1.	IRDP	14	21,000	14	7,298	33.3
2.	NABARD	15	75,000	–	–	–
3.	KVIC	17	1,24,750	17	45,375	44.0
4.	SC/ST	6	18,000	37	4,500	25.0
	Total	52	2,39,650	37	57,173	24.0

Source : Data compiled from Institutional Financing Agencies.

(xiii) Credit and Institutional Support

Institutional financing agencies operating in the district, who cater to the credit needs of rural artisans are namely, Co-operative Banks, Commercial Banks and Regional Rural Banks. As on 1989 the district is being served by 144 number of Commercial Banks, 100 RRBs, 33 branches of Central Co-operative Banks.

The Table 3.17 shows that, an amount of Rs. 4.18 lakhs of credit has been supplied to the sample artisans studied. Of which the share of Co-operative Bank, Commercial Banks and RRB constitute upto Rs. 1.04 lakhs, Rs. 1.13 lakhs, Rs. 2.0 lakhs, respectively. In terms of percentage the proportionate share of above mentioned institutions constitute 24.8, 27.2, and 48.0 per cent respectively. It shows that credit requirement of artisan units are mostly satisfied by Puri Gramya Bank, the Regional Rural Bank of the Puri district.

Table 3.17

Supply of Institutional Financing to Sample Artisan Units

(in Rs.)

	Sources	*Amount of loan supplied*	*% to the total*
1.	Cooperative Bank	1,03,750	24.8
2.	Commercial	1,13,400	27.2
3.	Regional Rural Banks/P.G.B.	2,00,600	48.0
	Total	4,17,750	100.0

Source: Data compiled from Institutional Financing Agencies, 1989.

However, the importance of other financing institutions may not be ignored. Due to increasing function of these institutions they are mostly engaged in financing the rural artisans in general and sample artisans in particular.

NOTES & REFERENCES

1. Government of Orissa, P & C Deptt. Directorate of S & E, *Statistical Outline of Orissa (1988-89)*, Cuttack, 1990.
2. Government of Orissa, P & C Department, *Economic Survey (1990-91)*, Directorate of S & E, Cuttack, 1992.
3. S.L.B.C., Orissa, UCO Bank, *20 Years of Bank Nationalisation (1989)*, Bhubaneswar, 1990.
4. Government of Orissa, P & C Deptt., S & E, *Economic Survey (1983-84)*, Cuttack, 1985.
5. Government of Orissa, *Economic Survey (1989-90)*, op.cit.
6. *Ibid.*
7. *Op. cit.*
8. NABARD, Bhubaneswar, Workshop for Development of Non-Farm Rural Sector, Reading Materials: (1990).
9. Mishra, D., "Cottage Industries in Puri District," *Orissa Review*, Government of Orissa, Cuttack, May 1988.

10. Government of Orissa, District Statistical Office, *District Statistical Hand Book*, Puri (1989-90), Cuttack, 1991.

11. Government of Orissa, Directorate of Agriculture and Food Production, *Orissa Agricultural Statistics (1989-90)*, Cuttack, 1991.

12. *Op. cit.*

13. Basudev Sahoo, *Weaker Sections*, 1984, Asish Publishing House, New Delhi, 1985.

14. Government of India, *Planning Commission Report of the Working Group on Khadi & Village Industries*, (September 1980), New Delhi, 1981.

15. Government of Orissa, Directorate of Industries, *Report of the Task Force on Handicrafts* (1977), BBSR, 1978.

16. Government of Orissa, Directorate of Textiles, *Agenda for ADT Meeting* (1988-89).

17. *Op. cit.*

18. G. Dash & S.N. Mishra, *RBI, A case study of Applique Artisans of Pipli* (1985), RBI Chair, Utkal University, 1985.

19. IDBI, *Consultancy and Development* (Dec. 1985), Bombay 1986.

4

Institutional Credit Structure for Rural Artisans: Organisation and Operational Policies

In the earlier chapter, an attempt was made to give a brief outline of the socio-economic background of Orissa economy in general and the economy of Puri district in particular. Besides, attention was also focussed on identifying the needs and requirement of rural artisans in the state and in the district. It is revealed from the foregoing discussion that of all the problems faced by rural artisans, lack of finance appears to be one of the main bottlenecks. As a matter of facts, finance is mostly supplied to the rural artisans from two sources, that may be categorised as institutional sources and non-institutional sources. A study of Reserve Bank of India in the year 1970-71 records that the rural artisans procure 92.6 per cent of their total credit requirement from non-institutional agencies. It is therefore, of immediate necessity to spread the network of institutional financing agencies, to cater to the needs of rural artisans. It is against this background that an attempt is made in this chapter, to make an overview of the institutional credit structure, existing for the rural artisans in the state.

The institutional credit structure mainly consists of institutions, such as; the Cooperative Banks, the Commercial Banks and the Regional Rural Banks. Characteristically, they are the purveyors of short term credit to the rural artisans. As against this, the rural artisans also procure credit from term lending institutions, like Orissa State Financial Corporation. The State Government mainly plays the role of a promotional agency, and is not directly involved in supplying cash finance to the artisan based units, except the fact that it administers subsidy to the different categories of borrowers in the countryside. An analysis of the institutional credit structure will reveal the relative performance of different institutions in the field of supplying institutional credit to the rural artisans in the state.

COOPERATIVE BANKS

Cooperative Banks the oldest institutional financing agencies in the state came into existence in the year 1904. Their progress was found more significant during different plan periods. The Cooperative Banks are classified into two categories such as; agricultural credit cooperatives who primarily deal with the farmers, and the non-agricultural credit cooperatives who deal with borrowers engaged in activities other than agriculture.

The agricultural credit coopervatives are again sub-divided into short-term credit cooperatives and long-term credit co-operatives. The short-term credit structure is federal in type. At the grass root level, i.e. at the village and block level there are Primary Agricultural Cooperative Credit Societies (PACS). At the apex level, there is the State Co-operative Bank, which is mostly located at the State Headquarter. In between there are Central Cooperative Banks, who act as the balancing centres between the State Cooperative Banks on the one hand, and PACS on the other. There are in Orissa nearly 17 Central Cooperative Banks. Thus, there occurs a two way flow of funds in the Cooperative Credit Structure. In one way State Cooperative Bank, from its own fund and also after receiving refinancing funds from NABARD, supply the same to the Central Cooperative Banks, who then in turn supply the same to the Primary Agricultural Co-operative Societies, for purpose of being lent to the ultimate members, the farmers. The members mostly constitute the farmers and the agricultural labourers. Only latter borrow credit for purpose of artisan units, which they adopt as subsidiary occupation. The primary agricultural co-operative societies mainly supply credit to the rural artisans at the rate of 10 per cent of rate of interest per annum. They are financed on the ground of having surity of all other co-members of the cooperative societies.

However in supplying credit to the rural artisans, PACS face certain problems. The credit is not supplied timely and in adequate quantity to the borrowers. Moreover failure to repay the loans in time has affected the PACS to claim assistance from higher financing agencies. Besides the PACS have also failed, to supply other facilities like, marketing, storage, supply of inputs, and training to the rural artisans.

The long term credit structure for agriculture in the state is of federal type. The long-term credit structure consists of Central Land Development Banks and Primary Land Development Banks. They provide mainly long-term credit to farmers. The rural artisans, virtually have no link with these agencies.

Non-Agricultural Cooperative Credit Societies

Most of the rural artisans, however, receive financial assistance from non-agricultural co-operative credit societies. These co-operative societies are : the Industrial Co-operatives like Khadi and Village Industrial Co-operative Societies, Primary Weavers Co-operatives Handicraft Co-operative Societies, Coir Co-operatives and Tassar/Mulberry Marketing Co-operative Societies. They mainly depend on Central Co-operative Bank and who in turn, depend upon its own fund and also on State Co-operative Bank, for financial accommodation. The State Co-operative Bank later get refinancing accommodation from NABARD. These industrial co-operative are mainly required to receive financial assistance from the Central Co-operative Banks. However, when they supply assistance to the artisans, they supply

Table 4.1

Status of Industrial Cooperative Societies in Orissa (1980-81 and 1988-89)

Year	*Khadi & Village Industries (OK, VIB) Societies*		*Handicraft Societies*		*PS/Units & Rural Industry Co-Op. Societies*		*Other Industrial Co-op. Societies*		*Total Industrial Co-Operatives*	
	No.	*Member-ship*	*No.*	*Member-ship*	*No.*	*Member-ship*	*No.*	*Member-ship*	*No.*	*Member-ship*
1980-81	624	27211	161	5034	95	3880	21	2661	901	38786
1988-89	634	34128	194	6160	73	2700	64	3200	965	46188
Percentage variation in 1988-89 over 1980-81	1.6	25.4	20.4	22.4	(-)23.2	(-)30.4	204.8	20.3	7.1	19.1

Source: Government of Orissa, Directorate of Industries, *Statistical Hand Book of Target and Achievement in SSI and Artisan Sector*, 1980-81 and 1988-89.

mainly in terms of raw materials, tools and equipments etc. The assistance takes the form of working capital assistance and term capital assistance. The loan is given through the industrial cooperative to the rural artisans at a rate of nine per cent per annum. At present, Industrial Cooperative Societies are required to make themselves registered in the respective District Industries Centres (DICs) which are functioning under the department of Directorate of Industries, Government of Orissa. Table 4.1 shows the growth and progress of industrial cooperative in the state, as they are being registered in various DICs in the State Government.

However, the growth of industrial co-operative societies shows a very discouraging trend. The number as well as membership has only increased by 7.1 and 19.1 per cent respectively, in 1988-89, over the figure of 1980-81. It thus reveals that there has been insignificant growth in the number as well as members over these years.

However, a large segment of the artisan units are seen to be functioning under these co-operative organisation in the state over all these years. The growth and progress of various types of artisan industrial co-operative societies are being discussed below.

Khadi and Village Industries Cooperative Societies

In the scheme of rural industrialisation Khadi and Village Industries has a vital role to play. Under Khadi and Village Industries a total number of 26 artisans based units have been included. The list comprising Khadi and Village Industries however have undergone significant changes in recent years. Now it contains 91 types of industrial units. Khadi and Village Industries have been looked after by the Khadi and Village Industries Commission, a statutory organisation of Government of India, established in the year 1953. At the state level, there are the KVIBs. In Orissa this KVI Board came into existence in the year 1957. At the village level there are the industrial co-operative societies, who are primarily responsible for the promotion and nurturing of Khadi and Village Industries. In order to look after the industries at the village and the block level, there are industrial promotion/extension officers appointed by State Government. They work in close liaison with Orissa Khadi and Village Industries Board (OKVIB).

Funds to the Khadi and Village Industry, are supplied by KVIC, out of the budgetary allocation of Central Government. Funds, then flow to KVIBs located in all states. KVIBs thereafter, allocate the fund to industrial co-operative societies, through the concerned bank at the Block. The Industrial Co-operative Societies supply the funds thereafter to individual artisans engaged in Khadi and Village Industries on the recommendation of DIC which is entrusted with the responsibility of identifying the deserving beneficiaries. Khadi and Village Industries are mostly located in rural areas having upto 10 thousand of population, and in semi-urban areas having upto 25,000 of population. Loans are usually given to the beneficiaries at a rate of 4 per cent per annum. Subsidy varying between 30 per cent and 50 per cent is provided to Khadi and Village artisans by the Government. It is further seen that artisan borrowers are not required to give any security for receiving loan upto Rs. 10 thousands. The borrowers are required to repay the loan within a period of five years, by equal instalments. The District Industries Centre (DIC) has got a close liaison with the industrial co-operative societies. Firstly, it undertakes the responsibility of identifying the artisans, in association with his co-operative societies. Secondly, DIC provides necessary training and facilitates of supervision and follow up action through Supervisors and Industrial Promotion Officers. At the same time, it also shoulders the responsibility of collecting statistical reports and returns about artisan based units, and forwarding the same to the Government.

Apart from finance, the marketing aspect of the societies is seen by the Artisan Industrial Multipurpose Co-operative Societies (AIMCS), located at the block level. At the district level, there are the District Level Gramodyog Marketing Co-operative Societies (DGMCS). It is the Central Cooperative Societies of KVIB, which is located at the district headquarter. Usually the AIMCS, gets the raw material and machinery and etc. from DGMCS, which in turn procure the same from KVIB. The AIMCS distributes the raw materials to the KVI artisans. The KVI artisans after producing the finished products, sale them to AIMCS who then markets the products through the DGMCS, through their show rooms opened in the districts. DGMCS also markets the products through KVIB sales Emporium located in urban centres and places outside the State. With this network of functioning KVIB has given a wide scope for growth and development of Khadi and Village Industrial Cooperative Societies which is shown in the Table 4.2.

Table 4.2

Progress of KVI Industrial Cooperative Societies in the State

(Rs. in lakhs)

Year	*No. of Coop. Societies*	*Investment*		*Production*	*Employment in No.*
		Grants	*Loans*		
1980-81	2181	21.13	171.76	735.52	65088
1988-89	3592	100.09	296.09	1735.91	89484
Percentage variation in 1988-89 over 1980-81	64.7	374.4	72.3	136.0	37.5

Source: Orissa Khadi and Village Industries Board, Annual Reports, 1980-81 and 1988-89.

The table reveals that the financing by OKVIB to the industrial co-operative societies in 1988-89 over 1980-81 have increased by 374.4 and 72.3 per cent in matter of grants and loans respectively. Side by side the number of cooperative societies as well as their production, and employment generation has also increased by 64.7, 136.0 and 37.5 per cent respectively over this period. Thus it shows that the growth and progress of KVI Industrial Cooperative Societies, is not quite encouraging.

Besides these Cooperative Societies, the progress of Artisan Industrial Multipurpose Cooperative Societies (AIMCS) as well as Gramodyog Marketing Co-operative Societies functioning in the state, is shown in Table 4.3.

Table 4.3

Achievement of Artisan Industrial Multipurpose Cooperative Societies (AIMCS) and Gramodyog Marketing Cooperative Societies (GMCS) in Orissa

(Rs. in Lakhs)

Year	*AIMCS Registered under DIC*	*Member*	*Working AIMCS*	*GMCS No. of sale outlet*
1980-81	209	12909	165	37
1988-89	150	12080	100	21
Percentage variation in 1988-89 over 1980-81	(-) 28.2	(-) 6.4	(-) 30.3	(-) 43

Source : Government of Orissa, Directorate of Industries, *Statistical Hand Book of Target and Achievement in SSI and Artisan Sector*, 1981-82 and 1988-89.

Table 4.3 shows that the number of AIMCs, its membership, number of working AIMCS and GIMCS sales outlet have declined over the period between 1980-81 and 1988-89 in the state.

It is revealed that though there exists quite a wide network of organisations for the growth and development of artisan industrial co-operative societies under OKVIB, the development of these societies is really not upto the mark. Due to conflict, confusion, and non-repayment etc. most of the societies are becoming dormant. With proper supervision and follow-up action, most of the problems of the societies will be checked, and they can be turn into active societies.

Weavers Cooperative Societies (WCS)

In the category of industrial cooperative societies, the Weavers Cooperative Societies occupy a significant position. These co-operatives are mainly provided with direct finance by the Central Co-operative Banks. The CCBs mainly get the required finance from SCB and which in turn get the fund refinanced by NABARD. NABARD fixes credit limit in respect of each CCBs who later draws the amount for purpose of supplying to Weavers Co-operative Societies functioning under production-cum-sale pattern. The weavers co-operative societies although receive finance from CCBs in cash yet while financing the weaver members, WCS makes it available in terms of raw materials. The finished product or handloom clothes are collected thereafter and the artisans are paid wages for manufacturing the product. Under this system both the raw materials as well as marketing need of weaver artisans are being satisfied. Since 1982 the NABARD is actively participating in this matter. And before that RBI was engaged in this activity. The Table 4.4 shows the financial accommodation provided by NABARD to the State Co-operative Bank and the fund which is sanctioned by the Central Co-operative Banks towards financing the weaving co-operative societies in the state since 1981-82 to 1988-89.

The Table 4.4 shows that over the years the cash credit limit sanctioned by NABARD has increased significantly. In the year 1981-82, Rs. 354.79 lakhs was being sanctioned and it had increased to Rs. 1,846.10 lakhs in 1988-89. Thus, it shows an increase of about 420.3 per cent over the amount sanctioned in 1981-82. It indicates that an increased amount is financed to the weavers co-operative societies. However, taking the figure related to total drawal allowed and the figures related to CCBs own financing in this regard, the progress shows a very distressing one.

Table 4.4

Cash Credit Limit Sanctioned by NABARD for Weavers Co-operative Societies

(Rs. in Lakhs)

Year	*Cash credit limit sanctioned by NABARD*	*Own fund sanctioned by CCB*	*Total*	*Total drawal allowed**
1980-81	354.79	65.26	420.05	571.25
1988-89	1846.10	–	1846.10	2262.41
Percentage variation in 1988-89 over 1981-82	420.3	–	434.7	296.0

* Total drawal is allowed to be 2.5 times of cash credit limit sanctioned by NABARD at a minimum.

– Indicates that in the year, the CCB has not financed credit to the weavers out of own fund.

Source: Government of Orissa, Directorate of Textiles, Bhubaneswar (Data mimeo).

It is revealed on principle that while sanctioning the cash credit amount, NABARD empowers the CCBs to advance atleast upto 2.5 times more of the total amount sanctioned by it. But is noticed that the total drawal has always remained less than that limit. It is due to the fact that the CCBs experience financial constraints. Accordingly the financing to Weaver Co-operative societies is also being reduced to that extent. A total of 10.5 per cent of rate of interest is charged by Central Co-operative Banks on Weavers Co-operative Societies for providing financial accommodation.

Besides these, to help the Weaver artisans functioning under Co-operative fold the State Government provide all the necessary infrastructure for a better marketing condition, through the Orissa State Handloom Weavers Co-operative Societies Ltd., (OSHWCS). It is noticed that though the primary societies are free to procure their own raw materials and arrange their own marketing, yet a major portion of their raw material collection and marketing, are carried out through this organisation. Orissa State Handloom Weavers Co-operative Societies thus supply the raw materials and collect the finished products and sale the same through its sales emporium, opened in the state and outside the state. The Directorate of Textiles, Government of Orissa, is the apex institution for control, management, monitoring and evaluation of the activities of Orissa State Handloom Weavers Co-operative Society Ltd. Due to active participation of OSHWCS in weaving sector the profit of the society has increased from 0.81 lakhs in 1974-75 to 85.00 lakhs in 1984-85.[1]

Moreover, due to active participation of NABARD, SCB/CCB and State Government, the number, production and employment generation by these WCS are increasing year after. This is seen from Table 4.5.

Table 4.5

Progress of Weavers Cooperative Societies in the State

Year	*No. of WCS working*	*Level of Production (in lakh Sq.mts)*	*Employment progressive (in actual Nos.)*
1980-81	514	228.00	75400
1988-89	750	586.51	162826
Percentage variation between 1980-81 and 1988-89	45.9	157.2	116.0

Source: Govt of Orissa, Directorate of Textiles (Data mimeo).

The table shows that the number of WCS which was 514 in the year 1980-81, had increased to 750 in 1988-89. The level of production has also increased from 228.0 lakh square mts of cloth to 586.5 lakh sq. mts and employment has increased from 75.4 thousand persons to 1.63 lakh persons in the year mentioned above. There has occurred an overall increase in number of societies by 45.9 per cent. Likewise production and employment increased by 157.2 and 116.0 per cent respectively between 1980-81 and 1988-89. It reveals that the growth and progress of WCS are quite remarkable. But the progress would have been much more if the financing to the sector would have been much more if the financing to the sector would have been properly made by SCB/CCB.

Handicraft Cooperative Societies

There are quite a large number of handicraft industries in the form of bell metal, applique and stone carving etc. found in the state. These are mostly labour intensive industries. They mostly use locally available resources and provide employment opportunities, in large number in the State. These products are highly artistic and possesses high aesthetic value. The products have a large local and foreign demand as well. The units are mostly operated by household enterprises. Not only the artisan, but his entire family are very often found to be working in these units.

Although there is the provision that the handicraft co-operative societies are to procure finance from Central Co-operative Banks located at district level, yet the supply of finance by CCBs is not very much encouraging. The handicraft co-operatives are mostly organised and promoted by the Department of Industry of the State Government and Orissa State Handicraft Corporation, which is also an organisation set up by the State Government. The Handicraft Co-operatives are being registered in the concerned DICs and are controlled by the Industry Department. However the State Government provides subsidy upto 25 per cent of the direct financing to handicraft artisans, made by financial institutions, on the ground of rehabilitation of handicraft artisan. Due to all these facilities available to the handicraft co-operative societies, there has taken place significant growth in number, production and employment generation of Handicraft Co-operative Societies. This is seen from Table 4.6.

Table 4.6

Progress and Performance of Handicraft Societies in the State

Year	*No. of Co-op. Societies*	*Membership (in No. of persons)*	*Employment (in No. of Persons)*	*Production (in lakhs)*
1980-81	181	5879	7000	240.00
1988-89	310	11215	17600	595.65
Percentage variation in 1988-89 over 1980-81	71.2	90.8	151.4	148.1

Source: Govt of Orissa, Directorate of Industries (Data mimeo).

The Table 4.6 shows that the growth of number of handicraft cooperative societies has increased from 181 in 1980-81 to 310 in 1988-89 showing a net addition of 129 new societies over the period. Percentage wise there had taken 71.2 per cent increase in the number of Handicraft Co-operative Societies, between 1980-81 to 1988-89. Besides, the membership, employment generation and production has also increased by 90.8 per cent 151.4 per cent and 148.1 per cent respectively. It shows that the growth of artisan units is quite significant in the state over these years.

Most of the handicraft products produced by these societies are being procured and marketed by Orissa State Handicraft Corporation since 1977. The Corporation is constituted out of the share capital contribution by the State Government and by the all India agency, like Development Commissioner of Handicrafts. The OSHC procures the products from source and is responsible for sale of the products in and outside the state and also in the overseas markets. Besides OSHC is also seen to be engaged in supplying raw materials to the bell metal co-operative societies since 1977. To undertake the scheme waste materials are collected by OSHC from various sources like Police Department and State Electricity Board etc. and ultimately those wastages are given as raw materials to the societies. The societies thus distribute this raw material among the artisans. OSHC later collects the finished product from the societies by paying the required wages.[2]

Thus with direct participation of OSHC, the Handicraft Co-operative Societies have made a significant progress. The Table 4.7 shows that during 1980-81 there was procurement and sale of Rs. 110.3 lakhs and Rs. 116.1 lakhs of handicraft products in the State by the Corporation. The amount has increased to Rs. 350.0 lakhs and Rs. 400.0 lakhs during the year 1988-89 respectively. It shows that there has been a growth upto 217.4 per cent and 244.6 per cent respectively between 1980-81 and 1988-89. It shows a significant increase in activities of handcraft co-operative societies and O.S.H.C.

Table 4.7

Procurement and Sale of Handicraft Items in the State by OSHC

Year	*Procurement (Rs. in lakhs)*	*Sale (Rs. in Lakhs)*	*Difference (Rs. in lakhs)*
1980-81	110.26	116.09	5.83
1988-89	350.00	400.00	50.00
Percentage increase in 1988-89 over 1980-81	217.4	244.6	757.6

Source : Government of Orissa, Office of OSHC., Bhubaneswar (Data mimeo).

For developing these units, State Government at times provides tools and subsidies etc. which is shown in Table 3.8.

Table 4.8

Subsidy/Free Tool Kit Given by State Government to Handicraft Artisans

Year	*Number*	*Amount (In lakhs)*
1980-81	371	1.35
1988-89	10	0.09
Percentage variation in 1988-89 over 1980-81	(-) 97.3	(-) 93.3

Source: Government of Orissa, Directorate of Industries, Cuttack, Statistical Hand Book of Target and Achievement in Small Scale and Artisan Sectors: 1980-81 and 1988-89 (Relevant issues).

It was noticed that in the year 1980-81, 371 units are assisted with Rs. 1.35 lakhs, whereas it has declined to only 10 units and 0.09 lakhs in 1988-89, showing a decrease of 97.3 per cent and 93.3 per cent respectively in 1988-89 over 1980-81.

Tassar/Mulberry Marketing Cooperative Societies

This industrial cooperative societies are also being organised in the state. They are mostly of three types like Tassar Marketing Cooperating Societies, Mulberry Rearers Co-operative Societies and Eri rearers co-operative societies. However, sericulture artisan societies are not very much popular in matter of Eri production in the state. It is observed that at present 62 Tassar Marketing Cooperative Societies, and 37 Mulberry Co-operative Societies are functioning in the state. Tassar type of sericulture is seen in districts like Mayurbahanj, Keonjhar, Sundargarh, Sambalpur, Dhenkanal, Cuttack and Balasore. The Mulberry, the new type of sericulture is becoming gradually popular in Koraput and Sambalpur. Eri type of sericulture is seen in Sundargarh and Phulabani districts. The State Tassar and Silk Co-operative Societies constitute the apex society, for all the Primary Sericulture Cooperative Societies. Besides providing marketing support to the societies, this apex society also provides credit to the primary cooperative societies. It is observed that a major portion of total financing to the primary societies is borne by the apex society. Besides these, the State Government with the collaboration of Central Silk Board is also catering to the credit needs of the Cooperative Societies on Sericulture. The Central Silk Board which is a central government organisation looks after growth and promotion of sericulture by providing training, seed supply, and undertaking research etc.

The growth and progress of Tassar marketing co-operative societies is shown below Table 4.9.

Table 4.9

Growth and Progress of Tassar Marketing Cooperative Societies

Year	*No. of Cooperative Societies*	*Production (1x1600)*
1980-81	62	11250
1989-90	62	22589
Percentage increase in 1989-90 over 1983-84	–	100.8

Source: Government of Orissa, Directorate of Textiles, Bhubaneswar, Data mimeo.

N.B.: Production is expressed in 'Kahan' = 1 x 1600.

Table 4.9 shows that the number of Tassar Marketing Co-operative Societies which was 62 in 1980-81 has remained the same in the year 1989-90 whereas the production of Tassar by these cooperatives increased from 11.3 thousand 'Kahan's as on 1980-81 to 22.6 thousand Kahans as on the year 1989-90. It reveals that there has been 100.8 per cent increase in production of silk in the aforesaid years. It may be said here that in the matter of silk collection from the societies, measurement is done through the unit 'Kahan' which is a traditional measuring yardstick, used for the purpose.

Coir Primary Cooperative Societies

Orissa is abundantly rich in coconut plantation. In the east coast of Orissa, beginning from Balasore to Ganjam there is mushroom growth of coconut trees. Consequently, this provides a good opportunity for establishing coir based industries in this region. In order to help and assist artisans working in the coir activities industrial co-operatives have been established for them. Usually coir artisans are the members of such societies. They are required to obtain financial assistance from Cooperative Banks, yet in practice the SCB/CCBs do not provide adequate finance to these societies.

The primary coir cooperative societies are mostly promoted by the Coir Board and by the State Government. The Coir Board is a Central Government organisation which is mainly organised for this purpose. These societies are being assisted by the Coir Board through the State Government. However, the fund is not available to the artisan co-operatives directly. It is disbursed through the DICs functioning in different districts. The Coir Board also provides marketing support to the artisan co-operative societies. However, for administrative purpose, State Government has included coir under the item called handicraft.

It was noticed that though there have been massive growth in the number of industrial co-operative societies in relation to various type of artisan units, their progress and performance have not been quite remarkable. Being democratic in nature the co-operative organisations generally suffer from their inherent weakness of conflict and confusion and local politics etc. Again due to the problem of non-repayment and mounting overdues the societies often become defaulters. Gradually they become sick and dormant. As a result of which they fail to get all the facilities from the co-operative banks and other organisations.

COMMERCIAL BANKS

On account of the inadequate role played by co-operatives to promote rural artisans, that a voice is mooted for the induction of commercial banks, for financing the rural artisans as a supportive or supplementary institution. The commercial banks have existed in the state for a long period of time.

It is however, observed that commercial banks, in their scheme of lending, primarily supplied credit to trade and commerce, and large industries. They did not lend any credit to sectors like agriculture, small scale industries, village and cottage industries, small business and retail trades etc., because they considered supplying finance to these sectors as a risky proposition. Moreover the Commercial Banks mostly concentrated their business activities in the urban and metropolitan areas. Following the dictum "Prosperity leads finance" the commercial banks, mostly concentrated their activities in the prosperous and lucky regions, where business prospects were brighter. As a result of this, a vast majority of population living in the countryside were deprived of getting organised banking facilities. Consequently they were left at the mercy of non-institutional agencies, where the moneylenders mostly dominated the scene.

The year 1969 is a landmark in the history of commercial banking in the country in general and state in particular. In this year 14 major commercial banks of the country, were brought under public ownership. On account of nationalisation, the commercial banks were asked to concentrate their activities more in the rural areas compared to urban and metropolitan areas. Besides expanding branch network in the rural areas the commercial banks were required to mobilise rural savings. Moreover, they are also required to deploy more credit to the hitherto neglected sectors like agriculture, small scale, village and cottage industries, small business and retail traders and professionally self-employed person. Commercial banks are required to dispense 40 per cent of their total credit, in favour of the designated priority sectors of the economy. Out of this priority sector advance again commercial banks are required to deploy 16 per cent of advance in favour of the agricultural sector and 10 per cent to scale, village and cottage industries. The balance was shared by all the other sectors belonging to the category of priority sectors.

In the scheme of priority sector financing the small scale and village and cottage industries occupy a significant position. The study conducted by RBI in the year 1957, accorded a greater role to these industries and suggested that the commercial banks should come forward in a large scale to finance these industries. In the year 1968 the National Credit Council in its Report "Organisational framework for the implementation of social objectives" categorically highlighted the existence of large-scale credit gaps in the hitherto neglected sectors wherein the village and cottage industries occupy an important position.

Accordingly since the nationalisation of banks in 1969 and 1980 the commercial banks have reoriented their activities with a view to serve the rural centres in general and the village and cottage industries in particular. It is seen that since 1969, the geographical and functional coverage of commercial banks in the rural areas have increased to a considerable extent.

Branch Expansion

It is found that since 1969 till the year 1989 the branch expansion of commercial banks in the rural centres has increased considerably compared to semi urban and metropolitan areas.

Table 4.10

Population Groupwise Distribution of Bank Branch Offices in Orissa Since 1972-89

	1972		*1989*		*Net increase in 1989 over 1972*	
Rural	90	(41.5)	610	(54.4)	520	(60.2)
Semi Urban	74	(34.1)	213	(19.7)	139	(16.1)
Urban/ Metropolis	53	(24.4)	258	(23.9)	205	(23.7)
Total	217	(100.0)	1081	(100.0)	864	(100.0)

Source : R.B.I., Banking Statistics, Basic Statistical Returns, 1972 and 1989, Bombay, pp.18 & 22.

Table 4.10 indicates that the number of branches has increased from 217 in 1972 to 1081 in 1989, showing a net addition of 864 branches over the period. Besides it is observed from the table that there has also taken place a significant growth of bank offices in Orissa particularly in rural centres. Bank offices in the rural centres as a percentage to total offices at the state level stood at 41.5 per cent and 54.4 per cent in the year 1972 and 1989 respectively. With the setting up of more bank offices in rural areas not only the borrowers will get an opportunity to come under the organised fold of banking but also it will help them to get rid of nefarious moneylenders who were earlier exploiting them.

Deposit Mobilisation

Another dimension of commercial banking activities in the rural areas is to mobilise the rural deposits as far as possible. The rates of interest on deposits have also been suitably revised upward in order to encourage the rural depositors.

Table 4.11

Population Groupwise Distribution of Deposits by Commercial Banks in Orissa, 1972 and 1989

(Rs. in lakhs)

	1972		*1989*		*Net increase in 1989 over 1972*	
Rural	5.89	(9.10)	42205.45	(21.3)	42199.66	(21.4)
Semi Urban	21.85	(34.6)	58756.14	(29.8)	58734.29	(29.8)
Urban/ Metropolis	35.36	(56.3)	96508.69	(48.9)	96473.14	(48.8)
Total	63.30	(100.0)	197470.28	(100.0)	197407.08	(100.0)

Source: RBI, Banking Statistics, B.S.R., 1972 and 1989, Bombay, pp.18 & 22.

N. B.: Figures in parentheses indicate per cent to the total.

Table 4.11 shows that of the total deposit mobilised in the state in 1972, the per cent share of deposit mobilised from rural areas was 9.1 per cent. However, the same increased to 21.3 per cent, in the year 1989 in the state. It reveals that the banking business has made a real break through in the rural areas in the matter of mobilising untapped resources.

Deployment of Credit

Another aspect of the functional coverage is deployment of credit. Since nationalisation the commercial banks are required to deploy a larger percentage share of the deposits, so collected from the rural areas, in the form of credit. The main purpose of such a need is to prevent the commercial banks in siphoning of scarce resources mobilised from the rural centres, for purpose of utilisation in the semi-urban and urban centres. Consequently this will help the commercial banks, to meet the credit requirements of vast number of population in the rural areas, who were earlier languishing for want of funds. It is seen from the following table that between 1972 and 1989 the banks have supplied quite a considerable amount of credit in the rural centres alone. This is seen by the fact that the credit deposit ratio in the rural centre has gone up quite considerably in 1989 compared to that of the year 1969.

Table 4.12

Population Groupwise Distribution of Credit in Orissa 1972 and 1989

(Rs. in lakhs)

Centres	*1972*	*1989*	*Net increase in 1989 over 1972*	*CD ratio in 1989 in %*
Rural	0.98 (3.4)	37003.63 (24.0)	37002.69 (23.9)	87.6
Semi-Urban	10.03 (35.0)	38688.16 (25.0)	38678.13 (24.9)	65.8
Urban/ Metropolis	18.05 (62.1)	79120.98 (51.0)	79102.93 (51.2)	82.0
Total	29.06 (100.0)	154812.77 (100.0)	154783.71 (100.0)	78.4

Source : R.B.I., Banking Statistics, Basic Statistical Returns, 1972 and 1989, Bombay, pp. 18 & 22.

N. B. : Figures in parentheses indicates per cent to the total.

It is observed from the Table 4.12 that the credit deployed by the commercial banks in the state has increased significantly. It also shows that, total credit advanced has increased from 29.06 lakhs to 1,54,812.77 lakhs showing a net addition of 1,54,783.71 lakhs between 1972 and 1989. It is seen from the table that whereas in 1972 the rural centres accounted for 3.4 per cent of total credit, the same stood at 24.0 per cent in 1989. Furthermore looking at net incremental credit between 1972 and 1989, it is noticed that whereas the rural centres accounted for 23.9 per of total incremental credit, the same for semi-urban and metropolitan areas were 24.9 and 51.2 per cent of the total. The data show that whereas in the state of Orissa the credit deposit ratio stood at 78.4 the same was 87.6 per cent in the rural centres in 1989. It is thus noticed that since nationalisation the bank credit was largely channelised in favour of rural centres which were previously deprived of the same. This seen from Table 4.12.

For providing credit, the commercial banks are now no more required to insist on for obtaining securities from the ultimate borrowers in the rural areas. The credit is now more need based and the commercial banks are required to channelise the credit for the purpose for which the credit is sought by the borrowers.

Supply of Credit to Village and Cottage Industries

It is seen that in the post-nationalisation period the share of village and cottage industries in the total credit to small scale sector has gone increasing. This is seen from the Table 4.13 given below.

Table 4.13

Distribution of Bank Credit to Village and Cottage Industries, 1972 and 1989

(Rs. in lakhs)

Year	*Financing to small scale sector*	*Share of village and cottage industries*	*% share to the total small scale sector financing*
1972	528	7	1.3
1989	12422	598	4.8
Net Variation	11894	591	
Percentage variation in 1989 over 1972	2252.7	8442.9	

Sources : (1) R.B.I., Bombay, Banking Statistics, Basic Statistical Returns, 1972 and 1982 and 1989 .

(2) 1989 Figs. UCO Bank, Regional Office, Bhubaneswar, (Data mimeo).

The table shows that in the year 1972, the supply of credit to small sector was Rs. 528 lakhs and the same increased to 12,422 lakhs in the year 1989. Over the period percentage increase in the small scale sector advance was upto 2,252.7 per cent. The table further indicates that in the year 1972 the supply of credit to Village & Cottage Industries by commercial banks was Rs. 7 lakhs. The same increased to 598 lakhs in 1989. The ratio of credit to village and cottage industries out of total small scale sector advance was 1.3 per cent and 4.8 per cent in 1972 and 1989 respectively which is not very much remarkable. However to advance credit to village and cottage industries sector, commercial banks have got a scheme of supplying credit to the rural artisans at a differential rate of interest of four per cent per annum. It may be observed that in order to provide finance to rural artisans and other small borrowers in the rural areas for enabling them to cross the poverty line, the Government has sponsored a number of programmes like IRDP, ERRP, NREP, RLEGP and TRYSM etc. For providing assistance under the scheme the government provides subsidy ranging between 25 per cent and 50 per cent.

REGIONAL RURAL BANKS

The working of commercial banks in supplying finance to rural artisans, as revealed from the previous sections clearly indicates that the banks have not supplied adequate amount of credit to rural artisans engaged in village and cottage industry sector. It is further noticed that whatever credit is supplied to borrowers, in the priority sector, that was mostly concentrated in the hands of the well-to-do amongst the small borrowers. In other words, the smallest amongst the small borrowers were deprived of getting adequate amount of bank credit, for purpose of pursuing their activities. Since, the rural artisans also come under this category, they have also not benefited much from this scheme of financing undertaken by the commercial banks.

Realising the dire necessity of small borrowers in

general, and the rural artisans in particular, it was suggested to have an alternative agency to cater to the needs of these borrowers. Accordingly the Government of India appointed a committee under the Chairmanship of M. Narasimhan, to look into the matter. The committee in its report suggested for the establishment of Regional Rural Banks in the country. Their areas of operation is mainly confined to the rural areas having less than 10 thousands of population. They mostly provide credit to the borrowers at a differential rate of interest of four per cent. The argument for such a low rate of interest is put on the basis of the fact that whatever loss the RRBs will incur on account of channelising credit at a concessional rate of interest will be made good, by commercial banks by charging high rate of interest, to well developed organised sectors. Public sector commercial banks are the sponsoring organisations of RRBs. In Orissa there are at present nine Regional Rural Banks covering almost all the 13 district of the state. In case of Orissa it is seen that two RRBs cover more than one district. A study of geographical coverage and functional coverage of RRBs will indicate their growing performance, between the year 1976 and 1989.

Branch Expansion

Since its inception the RRBs have taken a bold step to establish branches in the state. From 1976 to 1989, the branch expansion of RRBs has gone up by eleven times. The Table 4.14 shows the branch expansion of RRBs in the state between 1977 and 1989.

The table reveals that in the year 1977 RRBs opened 72 branches. This increased to 815 in the year 1989. Over the years there has taken place 1,032.0 per cent increase in the number of offices. Not only that, due to massive branch expansion the bank-branch ratio has also increased form 1:18 branches in 1977 to 1:90 branches in 1989. Furthermore, the ratio of village to RRB covered has also decreased from 735.7 in 1977 to 57.6 in 1989.

Table 4.14

Branch Expansion by RRBs 1977 and 1989

(Rs. in lakhs)

Year	*No. of RRBs*	*No. of Branches*	*Bank-Branch Ratio*	*Ratio of Villages Covered per RRB*
1977	4	72	1:18.0	735.7
1989	9	815	1:90.5	57.6
Percentage variation in 1989 over 1977	125.0	1032.0	402.8	

Sources: (i) RBI, Report of the Review Committee on RRBs, 1977 and 1989.
(ii) NABARD, Statistics on Regional Rural Banks, Bombay, 1980 and 1989.

It is observed that over the years, the RRBs have extended quite a large number of branches in the rural areas of the state. The objective of branch expansion was to provide organised banking facility at the door step of rural borrowers.

Deposit Mobilisation

One of the aspects of the functional coverage undertaken by RRBs relate to deposit mobilisation. Greater deposit mobilisation is considered essential to relieve the RRBs from depending on sponsoring banks for supply of funds. Furthermore, larger deposit mobilisation will assist the RRBs in meeting the credit needs of rural borrowers in a large scale. RRBs collect deposits under different schemes and pay rate of interest which is slightly higher than the rate charged by cooperative banks. The following table indicate the deposit mobilisation effort by RRBs.

Table 4.15

Deposit Mobilisation by RRBs, 1977 and 1989

(Rs. in lakhs)

Year	*No. of A/Cs*	*Amount of Deposits*	*Per capita rural deposits (Rs.)*
1977	30778	104.65	340.0
1989	1341676	11549.83	861.0
Net Addition	1310898	11445.18	521.0
Percentage variation in 1989 over 1977	4258.9	10828.0.	153.2

Sources: (i) RBI, Report of the Review Committee on RRBs, 1977.
(ii) NABARD, Statistics on RRBs, Bombay, 1980 and 1989.

The table shows that RRBs functioning in the state have mobilised 115.4 crores of deposits in the year 1989. However, this was 1.0 crores in the year 1977. This shows that net addition in deposit mobilisation over the years had been 114.5 crores. The number of depositors has also increased from 30 thousands in 1977 to 1,341 thousands in 1989. As a result of this per capita deposit increased from Rs. 340.0 in 1977 to Rs. 861.0 in 1989. It indicates growth and progress of RRBs in mobilising rural deposits.

Deployment of Credit

RRBs are engaged in supplying credit to the rural borrowers in general and the rural artisans in particular since their inception. For providing credit they charge a differential rate of interest of four per cent per annum and do not insist on securities, for sanctioning loan. The loan is mostly given on the basis of viability of the project which the artisans adopt. In a sense the RRBs mostly give need based credit. The credit is mostly given in the form of working capital. The performance of RRBs in relation to deployment of credit in general may be noticed from the following table (Table 4.16).

Table 4.16

Deployment of Credit by RRBs, 1977 and 1989

(Rs. in lakhs)

Year	*No. of Accounts*	*Amount (Rs.)*	*Per capita advance (Rs.)*	*Credit deposit ratio*
1977	30891	153.45	496.0	146
1989	1075307	19966.17	1857.0	173
Net Addition	1044416	19812.72	1361.0	
Percentage variation in 1989 over 1977	3381.1	1084.8	274.4	18.5

Source: *ibid*., Table 3.15.

The table shows that deployment of credit has increased from Rs. 1.5 crores to Rs. 199.7 crores during the period from 1977 to 1989. It reveals that the percentage variation in the amount of RRB credit in 1989 over 1977 was 1,084.8 per cent. Furthermore, between 1977 and 1989, number of borrowal accounts increased from 31 thousand to 108 thousand respectively. Consequently the per capita credit increased from Rs. 496.0 to Rs. 1,857.0 in the above mentioned years. Moreover, due to greater credit disbursement the credit deposit ratio which was 146.0 per cent in 1977 went upto 173.0 in 1989. It is needless to state that being rural based, the credit advanced by RRBs is mostly directed towards rural areas of the state.

Share of Rural Artisans in Total RRB Credit

The amount of credit supplied to the weaker section borrowers including the rural artisans is shown in Table 4.17.

Table 4.17

Financing to Rural Artisans Sector by RRBs in the State

(Rs. in lakhs)

Year	*Total RRBs finance*	*Share of rural artisans*	*% share of rural artisans of total RRB credit*
1981	3812.67	148.99	3.9
1989	19966.17	1540.04	7.7
Net Addition	16154.50	1391.05	3.8
Percentage increase in 1989 over 1981	423.7	933.7	

Source: NABARD, Bombay, Institutional Development Deptt. (RRB Division), *Quarterly Handout Report*, June 1981 and June 1989.

The table shows that financing by various RRBs has increased significantly in the state. While making a comparison between 1981 and 1989 figure, it reveals that financing as a whole has increased by 423.7 per cent in 1989 over 1981. Simultaneously it indicates that the percentage increase in this amount of RRB finance to rural artisans was 933.7 in 1989 over 1981. Furthermore, it is also noticed that the proportion of financing to the rural artisans to the total financing stood at 7.7 per cent in 1989, whereas it was 3.9 per cent in 1981. It shows that the percentage share has shown an increasing trend.

RRBs have also supplied credit under different schemes like IRDP, ERRP and others. However, it is noticed that financing under various schemes by RRBs have decreased in the recent year. The table below shows that the total amount of advance under the schemes has decreased from Rs. 4,361 lakhs in 1984 to Rs. 1,521 lakhs in 1989. Number of beneficiaries also decreased from 288 thousand in 1984 to

Table 4.18

Schemewise Distribution of Credit by RRBs in Orissa in 1984 and 1989

(Rs. in lakhs)

Year	*IRDP*		*DRI*		*Others*		*Total*	
	A/Cs.	*Amount*	*A/Cs.*	*Amount*	*A/Cs.*	*Amount*	*A/Cs.*	*Amount*
1984	86495	1516.01	31545	445.64	170300	2399.23	288340	4360.88
1989	49223	1141.26	3138	67.95	17822	311.94	70183	1521.15
Percentage variation in 1989 over 1984	43.1	10.2	90.1	53.1	89.5	87.0	75.7	65.1

Source : NABARD, Bombay, Institutional Development Deptt., RRB Division, *Quarterly Progress Report*, RRB, DEC. 1984, p. 11, March, 1989, p. 54.

70 thousand in 1989. It indicates that though amount of advance has increased in general, but financing under the schemes to rural artisans has not increased significantly. It is however, expected that RRBs need to involve themselves greatly in solving the problems of rural artisans. This is seen from Table 4.18.

NABARD

The Apex Bank for all the short-term credit institutions is the NABARD. It provides refinancing facilities to co-operative Banks, Commercial Banks and RRBs for undertaking the supply of finance to small borrowers including the rural artisans. The following Table 3.19 indicates the role of NABARD in providing refinancing facilities in Orissa between 1986 and 1989.

Table 4.19

Supply of Refinance Loans by NABARD in Orissa, 1986-1989

(Rs. in lakhs)

Year	*Total Refinance facilities*	
	Schematic Finance	*Unschematic Finance*
1986-87	43.12	86.82
1987-88	5022	104.34
1988-89	51.54	117.29
Percentage variation in 1989 over 1986	19.5	35.1

Source: NABARD, Statistical profile (Data mimeo).

The table shows that the refinancing to the state has been increasing over all these years. The schematic financing has increased by 19.5 per cent and unschematic finance has increased by 35.1 per cent in 1989 over 1986. As a result of increased refinancing facilities the institutional financing agencies have got the opportunity of supplying more credit to small borrowers including the rural artisans.

Orissa State Financial Corporation (OSFC)

Apart from the short term credit institutions, small borrowers including the rural artisans also receive assistance from Orissa State Financial Corporation (OSFC), which was established in the year 1956. Since its inception it has opened 17 branches covering 13 districts of the state. The OSFC is called upon to finance rural artisans under composite loan scheme in the year 1978-79. Under the scheme the artisan units are financed with a loan amount of Rs. 25 thousand. The Corporation provides both working and block capital to the artisans. The loans are given for a period of 7 to 10 years with a moratorium period of 12 to 18 months and with a rate of interest varying between 8.5 per cent and 10 per cent per annum. For the quick disposal of loan the Branch Managers are delegated with the power to sanction the credit without having any recommendation from DIC. Orissa Financial Corporation has also made tie up arrangement with OSHC (Orissa State Handicraft Corporation) and OHDC (Orissa Handloom Development Corporation) and Leather Corporation, for financing some particular type of artisans. The OSFC get refinancing facilities from Industrial Development Bank of India (IDBI) for providing credit to the rural artisans. The table 3.20 gives the role of OSFC in supplying credit to the rural artisans in the state.

The table shows that in the year 1979-80, OSFC supplied an amount of Rs. 84 lakhs to the rural artisans in the state. In the year 1989 the same stood at 5 lakhs. This shows that over the year there has taken place significant decline in the amount of OSFC finance to Rural Artisans. The same was also the case in the borrowal account, which declined from 1520 to 35 during the aforesaid period. It is mostly due to non-repayment and increased sickness among the artisan based units.

Table 4.20

Supply of Finance to Rural Artisans by OSFC, 1978-79 to 1988-89

(Rs. in lakhs)

Year	*Loan supplied to Rural Artisans*	
	No. of A/Cs	*Amount*
1979-80	1520	83.61
1988-89	35	4.99
Percentage variation in 1989 over 1984	(-) 97.7	(-) 94.0

Source: OSFC, Cuttack, Annual Reports, 1979-80, p. 16 and 1988-89 p. 50.

Multi Agency Approach

There is thus a multi agency approach to financing rural artisans in the state.

Table 4.21

Performance of Institutional Financing Agencies Supplying Finance to Rural Artisans in 1989 in Orissa

(Rs. in lakhs)

Institutions	*Amount outstanding*	*% share to the total*
1. Cooperative Banks	2658.59	55.4
2. Commercial Bank	598.00	12.4
3. Regional Rural Bank	1540.04	32.1
4. OSFC	4.99	0.1
Total	4801.62	100.0

Source: As cited in earlier tables.
For Co-operative Banks, See Table 4.2, 4.4, 4.8
For Commercial Banks, See Table 4.13
For RRB, See Table 4.17
For OSFC, See Table 4.20

It is noticed from the table that Co-operative credit structure have applied nearly 55.4 per cent to total institutional credit supplied to rural artisans in the year 1989. This is followed by Regional Rural Banks which supplied nearly, 32.1 per cent of the total institutional credit. The commercial banks supplied only 12.4 per cent of the total institutional credit in the year 1989 to rural artisans. As a matter of fact the share of OSFC is only 0.1 per cent of total institutional credit to rural artisans.

It is against this background that an attempt is made to study the performance of institutional financing agencies in supplying assistance to rural artisans in Puri district.

REFERENCES

1. Government of Orissa, Directorate of Textiles, Agenda for ADT Meeting, 1988-89.

2. Government of Orissa, Directorate of Industries (Handicraft Wing) Bhubaneswar, Task Force on Handicraft, 1977.

5

Working of Institutional Financing Agencies in Puri District

The Institutional Credit structure in Puri district consists of the following institutions such as, the Cooperative Banks, the Commercial Banks, Regional Rural Banks, and Orissa State Financial Corporation. Thus, an analysis of the existing institutional credit structure will reveal the relative performance of different institutional agencies supplying finance to the rural artisans in the district.

COOPERATIVE BANKS

Cooperative Credit Institutions constitute the oldest form of institutional financing agencies, functioning in the district for the growth and development of rural artisans.

The Cooperative credit institutions existing in the district depict the same structure that exist at the state level. It is noticed that while at the state level, there is the State Co-operative Bank, at the district level there is the Central Co-operative Bank. At present the Puri district is being served by three Central Co-operative Banks, namely, Nayagarh Central Cooperative Bank, Khurda Central Cooperative Bank and United Puri-Nimapara Central Cooperative Bank. As on 1989, these banks are having 12, 10 and 7 respectively of their branches spread all over the district at the block and Tahsil level. In the district there are 541 number of Primary Agricultural Co-operative

Societies (PACS) operating in the year 1986-87. However in the year 1981-82 the number of PACS was 529.[1]

As stated earlier, the PACs are mainly responsible for providing credit to the farmers and artisan borrowers. They provide finance in the form of cash and kind to the ultimate borrowers including the artisans. The performance of Co-operative banks in supplying credit through Primary Co-operative Societies to artisans is seen from the Table 5.1.

Table 5.1

Supply of Finance by Cooperative Bank to Rural Artisans in Puri District

(Rs. in lakhs)

Year	*Total credit financed (in lakhs)*	*Amount financed to Village and Cottage Industries (in lakhs)*	*% to the total credit by Cooperative Bank*
1980	803.03	15.05	1.8
1989	4258.17	423.55	10.0
Net variation in 1989 over 1980	3455.14	408.50	32.1

Source: UCO Bank*, Lead Bank Office, Puri District Credit Plan and Annual Action Plan for Puri District, 1980 and 1989.
* UCO Bank is the Lead Bank of the district.

The Table 5.1 shows that PACs at the district level are actively participating in financing the rural artisan units. It shows that the total supply of finance in the district, has increased by 3,455.14 lakhs in 1989 over 1980. And the supply of finance to artisan sector has increased by 408.5 lakhs during the aforesaid period. While 1.8 per cent of total financing has been made available to these units in the year

Table 5.2

Progress of Industrial Co-operative Societies in the District of Puri (As Registered in DIC)

(Rs. in lakhs)

Year	*No. of Industrial Co-operative Societies in working condition*					*Non-working Industrial Co-operative Societies*	*Total Co-operative Societies*
	KVI	*Handi-craft*	*PSI*	*Other*	*Total*		
1980-81	84	40	12	–	136 (35.0)	253 (65.0)	389 (100.0)
1988-89	70	60	12	15	157 (34.7)	295 (65.3)	452 (100.0)
Percentage variation in 1988-89 over 1980-81	(-)16.7	50.0	–	15.0	15.4	16.6	16.2

Source: Directorate of Industries, Statistical Hand Book of Target and Achievement of small scale and Artisan Sector, Cuttack 1981-82, p. 51 and 1988-89, pp. 68, 69.

1980, nearly 10.0 per cent of the total financing has been directed to these artisan units, in the year 1989.

Most of the artisans, however, receive financial assistance from Industrial Cooperative Societies, which are mostly of non-agricultural in nature. These industrial co-operatives are: Khadi and Village Industrial Cooperative Societies, Primary Weavers' Cooperatives Societies, Handicraft Cooperative Societies and Coir Cooperative Societies etc. This seen from Table 5.2.

Table 5.2 indicates that in the year 1980-81 there were 136 working industrial cooperatives and 253 non-working industrial co-operatives. The same increased to 157 working and 295 non-working industrial co-operatives in the year 1988-89. It is further revealed that out of this total industrial co-operative societies, the proportion of working co-operatives to total number of co-operatives stood at 35.0 and 34.7 per cent, respectively in 1980-81 and 1988-89.

Khadi & Village Industrial Cooperative Societies

Khadi and Village Industrial Cooperative Societies constitute the most important type of cooperative societies functioning for artisans at the district level. The terms and conditions regarding financing to the member artisans are the same as those exist at the state level.

The growth of Khadi and Village Industrial Cooperative Society is given in Table 5.3.

It is observed from the table that there were 199 industrial cooperative societies functioning in the district. The same however, increased to 741 in the year 1988-89. Percentagewise there has taken place an increase of 272.4 per cent over the period. The number of working cooperation society and the number of non-working cooperative societies and their production has increased by 145.7, 310.5 and 273.9 per cent respectively over the period. However employment had declined by 52.2 per cent in 1988-89 over 1980-81. This is due to reorganisational plans undertaken in KVI cooperatives.

Table 5.3

Progress of KVI Cooperative Societies in Puri District, 1980-81 and 1988-89

Year	*No. of Co-op. Societies*	*No. of Co-op. Societies in working condition*	*No. of Co-op. in non-working condition*	*Production (in crores)*	*Employ-ment (in Nos.)*
1980-81	199	46	153	2.02	24041
1988-89	741	113	628	7.55	11503
Percentage variation in 1988-89 over 1980	272.4	145.7	310.5	273.9	(-) 52.2

Source: OKVIB, Bhubaneswar, Annual Reports 1980-81 and 1988-89.

OKVIB is actively engaged in financing these artisan cooperatives and individual artisans as well. It is shown in Table 5.4.

Table 5.4

Financial Assistance by OKVIB to Artisan Cooperatives and Artisans in Puri District, 1980-81 and 1988-89

(Rs. in lakhs)

Year	*Co-operative*		*Artisans*		*Total*	
	No.	*Amount*	*No.*	*Amount*	*No.*	*Amount*
1980-81	58	30.64	103	0.98	161	31.62
1988-89	12	9.02	153	3.02	165	12.04
Percentage variation in 1988-89 over 1980-81	(-) 79.3	(-) 70.7	48.5	208.2	2.5	(-) 61.9

Source: OKVIB, Bhubaneswar, Annual Reports 1980-81 and 1988-89.

Table 5.5

Progress of AIMCS and GMCS in Puri District

(Rs. in lakhs)

Year	*Artisan Industrial Multipurpose Co-operative Societies*						*Gramodyog Marketing Co-operative Societies*		
	Regd. under DIC	*Member-ship*	*AIMCS effectively working*	*Value manufat-ured & article received for sale*	*Value sold*	*Value of raw materials supplied to artisans*	*No. of sales outlets*	*Value received for sale*	*value sold*
1980-81	35	1938	15	0.94	–	–	11	20.23	19.84
1988-89	2	70	2	0.98	1.05	–	1	12.24	10.85
Percentage (-)94.3 change in 1988-89 over 1980-81	(-) 96.4	(-)80.0	(+)4.3	(+)1.05	–	(-)90.9	(-)39.5	(-)45.3	

Source: Directorate of Industries, Government of Orissa, Target and Achievement under SSI and Artisan Sector, 1980-81 and 1988-89.

The Table 5.4 shows that financing by OKVIB to artisan co-operatives and individual artisans has not increased significantly. The number of units financed which was 161 in 1980-81, has increased to 165 showing an increase of 2.5 per cent in 1988-89 over 1980-81. Whereas the amount financed has declined from 31.62 lakhs to 12.04 lakhs over the period, showing a decrease of 61.9 per cent. It was noticed that number and amount of financing in case of artisan co-operatives had declined by 79.3 and 70.7 per cent respectively in 1988-89 over 1980-81, whereas the number of units financed and amount financed to artisan units have increased by 48.5 per cent and 208.2 per cent respectively over the aforesaid period.

For better implementation of its industrial programmes, OKVIB has established Artisan Industrial Multipurpose Co-operative Societies (AIMCS) at the block level, Gramodyog Marketing Co-operative Societies (GMCS) at the Sub-divisional level and District Gramodyog Marketing Co-operative Society (DIMCS) at the district level. The growth and performance of these AIMCS and GMCS are being shown in the Table 5.5.

The table shows that there were 35 Artisan Industrial Multipurpose Cooperative Societies in the year 1980-81, whereas it declined to only two in the year 1988-89. The total membership which was 1938 in 1980-81, was only 70 in 1988-89. However, the value manufactured and articles received for sale and value actually sold have increased by 4.3 per cent and 1.1 per cent respectively over the aforesaid period. The number of Gramodyog Marketing Cooperative Societies which was 11 in 1980-81 has declined to only one in 1988-89. Not only that the value received for as well as value of articles actually sold has declined by 39.5 and 45.3 per cent respectively, over the period.

Weaver Cooperative Societies (WCS)

The weaver cooperative society occupies a significant position both in the state as well as in the district. These societies are directly financed by the District Central Co-operative Bank (DCCB). And DCCB in turn avails refinancing facility from the NABARD. The term and procedures of financing to the weaver artisans remained the same as it is prevailing at the state level. The Central Co-operative Banks of the district like Puri, DCCB, Khurda and Nayagarh shoulder the responsibility of financing the weaver artisans, functioning under various Primary Weavers' Co-operative Societies (WCSs). These WCS are functioning mostly, on production-cum-sale basis. The progress of Weaver's Cooperative Societies in Puri district during the period from 1980-81 to 1988-89, is shown in Table 5.6.

Table 5.6

Growth and Progress of WCS in the Puri District 1980-81 and 1988-89

Year	*No. of WCS (Working)*	*Level of Production (lakh in sq.mtrs.)*	*Employment (cumulative in actual Nos.)*
1980-81	79	88.26	17032
1988-89	143	158.81	28262
Net Variation	64	70.55	11230
Percentage variation in 1988-89 over 1980-81	81.0	79.9	65.9

Source: Government of Orissa, Directorate of Textiles (Data Mimeo)

The table shows that the number of Cooperative Societies increased from 79 in 1980-81 to 143 in 1988-89. It shows a net addition of 64 new Co-operative Societies over the years. In percentage terms, the variation in 1988-89 over 1980-81 was 81.0 per cent. The level of production has also increased from 88.26 lakh square metres in 1980-81 to 158.81 lakh square mtrs. in 1988-89. Furthermore, the number of employment which was 17 thousand in 1980-81 has increased to 28 thousand in 1988-89, showing a net addition of 11 thousand persons over these years. Percentagewise both the production and employment increased by 79.9 and 65.9 per cent between 1980-81 and 1988-89.

The growth in the number of WCS and their production and employment generation are mostly caused by increased finance supplied to both by CCBs and NABARD. While NABARD provides the refinancing facilities, CCBs provide direct finance to WCS. The performance of NABARD and CCB in this respect is shown in Table 5.7.

Table 5.7

Flow of Fund by NABARD and CCB to the Weavers Cooperative Societies in Puri District

(Rs. in lakhs)

Year	*Cash Credit limit sanctioned by NABARD*	*Own fund sanctioned by CCB*	*Total*	*Total drawal*
1981-82*	100.10	15.05	115.55	205.15
1988-89	337.10	–	337.10	420.75
Percentage variation in 1988-89 over 1980-81	236.8	15.1	192.7	105.1

Source: Government of Orissa, Directorate of Textiles (Data Mimeo)
– Indicates nil financing in that year.
* Cash credit sanctioned by RBI.

The table shows that the cash credit limit sanctioned by NABARD was 100.0 lakhs in 1981-82. This has increased to 337.10 lakhs in 1988-89. The percentage variation was 236.8 per cent over the period. The table further indicates that the amount supplied by CCBs to WCS is not regular. In 1988-89 there was no supply of credit. Looking at the total advance, it is noticed that in the year 1981-82, a sum of Rs. 205.15 lakhs has been allowed to be drawn, whereas, it increased to Rs. 420.75 lakhs in 1988-89. It shows about 105.1 per cent increase in 1988-89 over 1981-82. However, according to the National Bank's stipulation total drawal should always be atleast more than 2.5 times of this amount of cash credit sanctioned by NABARD. But it is noticed that it has remained less than that both in 1981-82 and 1988-89.

Handicraft Cooperative Society

The district possesses an important place in the field of handicrafts like bell metal, stone carving, applique and patta chitras etc. It is noticed that the artisans engaged in the production of handicraft items are seen to be working either individually or through the co-operative societies. However, handicraft artisans, operating through handicraft co-operative societies is quite large. Handicraft Cooperative Societies are mostly functioning under the Directorate of Industries of State Government. As stated earlier, they are registered under DIC operating at the district level. These societies are required to be financed by the State and Central Cooperative Banks, but it is noticed that co-operative banks, rarely finance other industrial cooperatives including handicraft artisans. In the past the State Government was directly engaged in financing the handicraft artisans through the Handicraft Cooperative Societies. But due to misutilisation, non repayment and non-functioning etc. the scheme was discontinued. The State Government at present also provides raw material assistance to some specific category of handicraft artisan cooperatives. As for example, raw material banks are being opened on experimental basis for the bell metal cooperatives at certain places of the district like, Balakati, Bainchua and Kantilo etc. In these places the cooperatives engaged in bell metal craft are being supplied with raw materials. The finished products are thereafter collected from artisans for purpose of marketing. The artisans are paid due wages for producing the product. In the Puri district these bell metal cooperatives are seen to be actively functioning. The State Government through Orissa State Handicraft Corporation is also seen to be actively engaged in supplying raw materials to the rural artisans. The Table 4.8 shows the supply of subsidy/tools and kits to handicraft co-operatives and artisans in Puri district by the State Government.

Table 5.8

Supply of Subsidy/Free Tool Kit Given by the State Govt. of Handicraft Artisans in Puri District

(Rs. in lakhs)

Year	*No.*	*Amount*
1980-81	6	0.22
1983-84	13	0.39
Percentage variation in 1983-84 over 1980-81	116.0	(-) 77.3

Source: Government of Orissa, Directorate of Industries, Statistical Hand Book of Target and Achievements in Small Scale and Artisan Sectors from 1980-81 to 1983-84 (Relevant issues).

The table shows that State Government is not actively participating in financing the handicraft artisan units in the district. It shows that 6 artisan units were financed Rs. 0.22 lakhs in 1980-81, and the supply of subsidy and other tools and kits have continued till the year 1983-84. In the said year 13 units were being financed 0.39 lakhs. However, the assistance mostly stopped in the subsequent years.

Besides this it is to be noted that the procurement and sale of handicraft products are done by the Orissa State Handicraft Corporation (OSHC) operating in the district. The Head Office of this Corporation is located at Bhubaneswar. The OSHC thus shoulders the responsibility of selling the handicraft products in and outside the state through the approved show rooms and sales emporiums popularly known as Utkalika.

Coir Cooperative Societies

Since Puri district is one of the coastal districts of the state there are a large number of Coir-Co-operative Societies functioning in the district. The growth and promotion of coir cooperative societies are mostly looked after by the Directorate of Industries and by the State Government. The provision of financing to the Coir Cooperatives is almost same like that of the handicraft societies as discussed earlier. However, Coir Board, which is a Central Government agency is also catering to the financial needs of Coir Cooperatives through the State Government. The State Government for administrative point of view includes Coir Cooperative societies under the category of Handicraft Co-operatives.

In the district almost all the types of artisan cooperative societies are visible except that of sericulture. It is to be noted that sericulture as an artisan based industrial unit is not much developed in the district.

It may be observed that though there has taken place an increased need for funds in the artisan units operating in the district, yet the expansion of artisan cooperative societies has not made any significant improvement.

COMMERCIAL BANKS

Next to Cooperative banks are the Commercial Banks who work as supplementary institutions to cater to the needs of rural artisans. Since the nationalisation, the Commercial Banks have made an increased effort to extend the business activities in the rural areas of the district. Both in respect of geographical coverage and functional spread, the performance of commercial banks during the post nationalisation period is quite significant.

Branch Expansion

Since the year of nationalisation, bank branches have been opened all over the district. Looking at the branch expansion, it is noticed that commercial banks have opened more branches in the rural areas of the district. It is revealed from Table 4.9 that there were only 28 branches of commercial banks in the district, in the year 1972. This increased to 150 in the year 1989, percentwise, the increase was 435.7 per cent over the period. It is further revealed that in the year 1972 there were only 11 rural bank offices in the district. This increased to 71 bank offices in the year 1989. There is thus a net increase of 60 branches over the period. Percentwise distribution of rural branches account for 39.3 of the total in the year 1972. However, in the year 1989, the percentage distribution was 47.3 per cent. Compared to rural branches, the distribution of bank offices in semi urban and urban/metropolitan centres whereas stood at 7 and 10 respectively in 1972, the same was 10 and 69 in 1989. Percentagewise, the semi-urban and urban/ Metropolitan centres whereas accounted for 25.0 per cent and 35.7 per cent of the total in 1972, the same was 6.7 per cent and 46.0 per cent of the total respectively in 1989.

Table 5.9

Population Groupwise Distribution of Branch Offices of Commercial Banks in Puri District, 1972-1989

(Rs. in lakhs)

Year	*June 1972*	*June 1989*	*Net increase in 1989 over 1972*
Rural	11 (39.3)	71 (47.3)	60(49.2)
Semi-urban	7 (25.0)	10 (6.7)	3 (2.5)
Urban/Metropolies	10 (35.7)	69 (46.0)	59 (48.4)
Total	28 (100.0)	150 (100.0)	122 (100.0)

Source: 1972 figures, RBI, BSR, 1972, December, Vol.1, pp. 18 & 19.
1989 figures, Office source of,Lead Bank Office, UCO Bank, Puri.
(Data mimeo)
Figures in brackets indicate percentage to the total.

Over the period, the net increase in rural branches whereas stood at 60, the same was 3 and 59 respectively for semi-urban and urban and metropolitan areas. Percentagewise, the rural branches whereas accounted for 49.2 per cent of the total, semi urban and urban/metropolitan centres accounted for 2.5 per cent and 48.4 per cent of the total respectively between 1972 and 1989. The table further indicates that though the percentage distribution of rural bank offices increased in the district over the period, the percentage distribution of urban/metropolitan branches still continues to be the largest. Larger expansion of rural branches further indicates that the rural people have greater chance to avail banking facility in a greater magnitude than before. Furthermore, they will come under the fold of organised banking.

Deposit Mobilisation

To mobilise the rural deposits as far as possible the commercial banks have tailored suitable schemes and have revised the rates of interest. As a result of which the deposit mobilisation has not only increased in the district, but this has also helped to promote saving habit amongst the people in the rural areas (Table 5.10).

Table 5.10

Population Groupwise Distribution of Deposit Mobilisation

(Rs. in lakhs)

Centres	*1972*	*1989*	*Net increase between 1972 & 1989*
1. Rural (4.13)	0.57 (20.1)	11388.2 (20.1)	11382.5
2. Semi Urban (16.17)	2.23 (22.8)	12917.9 (22.8)	12895.6
3. Urban/ Metropolies	10.99 (79.69)	32351.5 (57.1)	32241.6 (57.0)
Total	13.79 (100.0)	56657.6 (100.0)	56519.7 (100.0)

Source: 1972- RBI, BSR, December 1972, Vol.I, pp. 18 & 19.
1989-UCO Bank, Lead Bank Office, Puri. (Data mimeo).
Figures in brackets indicate percentage to the total.

The Table 5.10 shows that the total amount of deposit mobilised from the district has increased from Rs. 13.79 lakhs in 1972 to Rs. 56,657.6 lakhs in 1989. The total deposit mobilisation from rural areas has increased from Rs. 0.57 lakhs in 1972 to Rs. 11,388.2 lakhs in 1989.

In the percentage, term, the proportion of rural saving to total saving which was 4.13 in 1972 stood at 20.1 in the year 1989. It shows commercial banks functioning in the district have actively engaged themselves in the mobilisation of deposits from the rural areas. Compared to rural areas, the deposit from semi urban and urban/metropolitan areas whereas accounted for 16.2 per cent and 79.7 per cent in 1972, the same was 22.8 per cent and 57.1 per cent respectively in 1989. This indicates that the semi-urban and urban/metropolitan areas together now account for the bulk of the deposits mobilised by commercial banks. Looking at net increase in the amount of deposits mobilised by commercial banks between 1972 and 1989, it is noticed that the rural branches, whereas accounted for 20.1 per cent of total deposits, the semi urban and urban/metropolitan centres accounted for 22.8 per cent and 57.0 per cent respectively of the total between the aforesaid period.

Deployment of Credit

The most important aspect of the functional coverage by commercial banks is the deployment of credit. Since nationalisation, the commercial banks have been motivated to deploy a major portion of the deposits. According to the stipulation of Reserve Bank of India, the commercial banks are required to deploy in the rural centres upto 60 per cent of their total deposits so collected from these centres. This target is to be achieved by 1985. The objective is to supply adequate amount of credit in the rural areas. The distribution of credit by commercial banks in different population groupwise centres is shown in the Table 5.11.

The Table 5.11 shows that the total credit advanced in the district has increased from Rs. 5.54 lakhs in 1972 to Rs.

Table 5.11

Population Groupwise Deployment of Credit by Commercial Banks in Puri District

(Rs. in lakhs)

Centres	*1972*	*1989*	*Net increase in the amount of credit between 1972 and 1989*	*Credit deposit ratio in 1989*
Rural	0.16 (2.9)	10599.99 (20.7)	10599.83 (20.7)	107.43
Semi-urban	0.69 (12.45)	9575.83 (18.7)	9575.14	134.90 (18.7)
Urban/ Metropolies	4.69 (84.6)	31031.86 (60.6)	31027.17 (60.6)	95.92
Total	5.54 (100.0)	51207.68 (100.0)	51202.14 (100.0)	90.38

Source: 1972- RBI, BSR, December 1972, Vol.I, PP.18 & 19.
1989-UCO Bank, Lead Bank Office, Puri, (Data Mimeo)
Figures in brackets indicate percentage to the total

51,207.68 lakhs in 1989. This indicates that commercial banks have supplied quite a large amount of credit in the district. It is further observed from the table that commercial banks deployed 0.16 lakhs in the rural centres in the year 1972. This increased to Rs. 10,599.9 lakhs in the year 1989. As against this the semi-urban and urban/metropolitan centres whereas accounted for Rs. 0.69 lakhs and Rs. 4.69 lakhs in the year 1972 the same was Rs. 9,575.8 lakhs and Rs. 31,031.9 lakhs respectively in the year 1989. Percentagewise, the rural branches whereas accounted for 20.7 of total advance the same was 18.7 and 60.6 of the total in semi – urban/metropolitan centres, respectively in the year 1989. In 1972, the percentage distribution of credit in rural centres was only 2.9 of the total. As against this, the semi-urban and urban/metropolitan branches accounted for 12.5

per cent and 84.6 per cent of the total respectively in the aforesaid year. It is, thus seen that the percentage distribution of rural credit has gone on increasing since the nationalisation of banks. It is revealing to note that inspite of the higher percentage increase in the distribution of credit in the rural area, the semi-urban and urban/metropolitan areas still account for the largest concentration of credit.

However, credit deposit ratio in the rural areas whereas stood at 107.4, the same was 134.9 and 95.9 in semi-urban and urban/metropolitan areas respectively in the year 1989. Higher credit deposit ratio in rural areas indicates that commercial banks have succeeded in fulfilling the target laid down by RBI with regard to deployment of credit i.e. 60 per cent of credit deposit ratio in rural areas by 1985.

Distribution of Credit in Favour of Village and Cottage Industries

The performance of the commercial banks in the district regarding sectoral distribution of credit reveals that, the banks have mostly financed according to the guidelines issued by the RBI. According to the instruction of RBI, of the total loan advanced, 40 per cent is required to be channelised towards the priority sectors.

It is noticed that commercial banks have supplied credit to the rural artisans at a differential rate of interest (DRI) of four per cent per annum. The available data show that commercial banks functioning in the district has given 122.10 lakhs, towards DRI advances in 1982, it stood at 731.60 lakhs in 1989. In terms of percentage the amount of loan advanced on DRI scheme out of the total lending by commercial banks whereas stood at 1.2 in 1982, the same was 1.6 in 1989.[1]

It is observed from Table 5.12 that the total amount of advance supplied by commercial banks to village and cottage industries was Rs. 0.65 lakhs in 1972. The same increased to Rs. 672.00 lakhs in 1989. It shows a variation of Rs. 671.35 lakhs. Furthermore, the village and cottage industries whereas accounted for 0.3 per cent out of total bank credit in 1972, the same was 1.3 per cent in 1989. This indicates that the percentage distribution of credit by commercial banks in favour of village and cottage industries has improved no doubt but the increase was marginal only.

Table 5.12

Supply of Bank Credit to the Village and Cottage Artisans in Puri District, 1972 and 1989

(Rs. in lakhs)

Year	*Total Bank Credit (Cumulative)*	*Share of Village & Cottage Industries (Cumulative)*	*% to the total Bank Credit*
1972	251.01	0.65	0.3
1989	51207.68	672.00	1.3
Net variation in 1989 over 1972	50956.67	671.35	

Sources: (i) 1972 Figs. RBI, Banking Statistics. Basic Statistical Returns.
(ii) 1989 Figs. UCO Bank, Regional Office, Bhubaneswar (Data mimeo).

Schemewise Distribution of Credit

The performance of commercial banks with regard to allocation of funds in favour of rural artisans on Government sponsored schemes is quite significant. The schemes under which the commercial banks are financing the rural artisans, are IRDP, ERRP, TRYSEM and DRI etc. The primary objective of these schemes is to enable the rural artisans to acquire assets in order to earn an income to overcome poverty. It is thus seen that in the post nationalisation period, the commercial banks have gone to a considerable extent in assisting the village and cottage industrial workers in the district. However, it is noticed that out of the total amount of loan advanced to the artisan sector, a major portion of it has gone to well-to-do amongst the rural artisans. Consequently, an alternative agency exclusively catering to the needs of small borrowers and rural artisans was mooted.

REGIONAL RURAL BANKS

Puri Gramya Bank came into existence in the year 1976. Since it is the oldest RRB established in the state, its growth and performance in the district is worth mentioning. The working and performance of Puri Gramya Bank are discussed below :

Branch Expansion

The Branch expansion of Puri Gramya bank has increased considerably over the years. This is observed from Table 5.13.

Table 5.13

Branch Expansion of Puri Gramya Bank in the District Puri, 1976 and 1989

Year	*No. of branches*	*Average population served per branch [in 000s]*
1976	20	131
1989	100	29
Variation in 1989 over 1976	80	102

Sources: (i) 1976 figures, Puri Gramya Bank, Head Office, Pipli (Data mimeo)
(ii) 1989 figures, NABARD, Institutional Development, RRB Division, *Quarterly Progress Report of RRBs*, 1989.
(iii) Government of Orissa, District Statistical Hand Book, 1989-90, Puri, DSO, Puri, PP.3 & 82.

It is seen from the table that in the year 1976, Puri Gramya Bank had opened 20 bank offices in the district, which increased to 100 in the year 1989. Over the years, a net increase of 80 branches have taken place in the district. Average population served per branch whereas stood at 131 thousands in 1976, the same came down to 29 thousands in 1989. This indicates that now a bank office of Puri Gramya Bank caters to the need of a smaller number of people than before.

Deposit Mobilisation

One of the functional aspects covered by Puri Gramya Bank, refers to deposit mobilisation. The performance of Puri Gramya Bank in this regard is quite encouraging. It is noticed that the deposit mobilised by PGB from the district has increased from Rs. 85 lakhs in 1977 to Rs. 1,628.0 lakhs in 1989. Not only that, the number of depositors have also increased from 20 thousand in 1977 to 154 thousand in 1989 showing a net addition of 134 thousand depositors over the period. Due to increase in the number of borrowal accounts and amount of deposits in PGB, the deposit per account has increased from Rs. 297 in 1977 to Rs. 1,057 in 1989, showing a net increase of Rs. 760 over the years. Per capita deposit has also increased from Rs. 3.3 in 1977 to Rs. 56.1 in 1989, an increase of Rs. 52.8 over the period. Performance of Puri Gramya Bank in the field of deposit mobilisation is shown in Table 5.14.

Table 5.14

Mobilisation of Deposits by Puri Gramya Bank 1977 and 1989

Year	*Deposit (No. of A/Cs)*	*Amount (in lakhs)*	*Deposit per A/C (in Rs.)*	*Per capita deposit (in Rs.)*
1977	20219	85	297	3.3
1989	154062	1628	1057	56.1
Net variation in 1989 over 1977	133484	1543	760	52.8

Sources: (i) 1972 Figs., Puri Gramya Bank, Head Office, Pipili, Annual Report.

(ii) 1989 Figs. NABARD, Institutional Development Deptt. RRB Division, *Quarterly Progress Report of RRBs*.

Deployment of Credit

The amount of credit advanced by Puri Gramya bank in the district has also gone up considerably during the period from 1977 to 1989. This is observed from Table 5.15.

Table 5.15

Deployment of Credit by Puri Gramya Bank

Year	*Advance (No. of A/Cs)*	*Advance (in lakhs)*	*Advance per A/C (in Rs.)*	*Per capita Advance (in Rs.)*	*Credit deposit ratio*
1977	15327	101	660	3.9	120
1989	114507	2857	2495	98.6	175
Variation in 1989 over 1977	99180	2756	1853	94.7	55

Sources: (i) 1977 Figures, Puri Gramya Bank, Head Office, Pipli, Annual Report
(ii) 1989 Figs. NABARD, Institutional Development Deptt. RRB Division, Quarterly Progress Report of RRB.

It is observed from the table that the amount of advance by PGB stood at Rs. 101 lakhs in 1977. This increased to Rs. 2,857 lakhs in 1989. During this period, the number of borrowal accounts increased from 15 thousand in 1977 to 114 thousands in 1989. Over the period variation in the number of accounts was 99 thousand. As a result of this, advance per account whereas stood at Rs. 660 in 1977, the same increased to Rs. 2,495 in 1989, Likewise, per capita advance during this period also increased from 3.9 to Rs. 98.6, respectively. Credit deposit ratio as an index of measuring the utilisation of fund by RRBs in the rural centres stood at 120 per cent in 1977 and 175 per cent in 1989.

As stated earlier the credit is mostly given without any security, and moreover loan is given with a low rate of interest. As a result of which amount of credit advanced has shown an upward trend over the years.

Sectoral Allocation of Credit

RRBs mainly provide credit to the weaker section borrowers. The amount of credit supplied to the weaker section borrowers including the rural artisans is shown in the Table 5.16.

The table shows that between 1981 and 1989, there has been a significant increase in the amount of credit advanced to rural artisans out of the total advance made by PGB. In the year 1989, an amount of Rs. 117.0 lakhs was advanced to the artisan units in the said year. In 1981 however the amount advanced to rural artisans stood at 20.64 lakhs. It thus shows that a net addition of Rs. 96.63 lakhs. This indicates that over the years the percentage variation in the amount of credit to rural artisans was 466.9. As a percentage to total advance made by PGB in the district, the share of advance going to Rural artisans was 2.6 per cent and 4.3 per cent respectively in 1981 and 1989. In comparison to other sectors, the percentage distribution of credit to rural artisans is low. Sectors like agriculture, allied and retail trade, small business including self employed persons had availed 65.5 and 36.5 per cent of the total loan advanced in 1981. The percentage share of both these sector to the total advanced stood at 39.9 and 44.0 per cent respectively in 1989. Hence, there is the necessity for providing further more advance to artisan sector.

Schemewise Distribution of Credit

Puri Gramya Bank like all other RRBs has also advanced credit to the artisan units under various schemes. The industrial advances coming under various schemes is mostly undertaking with the active participation of institutions like DIC, DRDA and Lead Bank. Available data show that the financing under beneficiary oriented schemes by PGB has increased in the recent years. In the year 1984, about 7,280 persons were covered under the schemes and they were advanced an amount of Rs. 165.53 lakhs. The figures stood at 16,626 persons and 402.02 lakhs in 1989. It

Table 5.16

Purposewise Classification of Direct Advances Outstanding by Puri Gramya Bank 1981 and 1989

(Amount in lakhs in Rs.)

Year	*Agril. & Allied*		*Rural Artisans*		*Retail Trade, Small Business including self employment*		*Consumption loan*		*Other Purpose*		*Total No. of A/Cs*	*Total Amount*
	No. of A/Cs	*Amount*	*No. of A/Cs*	*Amount*	*No. of A/Cs*	*Amount*	*No. of A/Cs*	*Amount*	*No. of A/Cs*	*Amount*		
1981	39838 53.8)	442.35 (65.5)	2100 (2.83)	20.64 (2.59)	30400 (41.05)	290.87 (36.5)	205 (0.27)	0.91 (0.11)	1503 (2.02)	41.30 (5.18)	74046 (100.0)	796.87 (100.0)
1989	41419 (36.1)	1078.00 (39.9)	5568 (4.86)	117.00 (4.33)	56950 (49.73)	1188.00 (44.03)	329 (0.28)	1.00 (0.03)	10198 (8.9)	314.00 (11.63)	114507 (100.0)	2698.00 (100.0)
Percentage increase in 1989 over 1981	84.0	143.7	165.1	466.9	87.3	308.4	60.4	9.9	625.1	660.3	54.6	238.6

Sources: (1) 1981 figure : RBI Central office, Bombay (Data mimeo)
(2) 1989 figures : NABARD, Bombay, Institutional Development Department, RRB Division, Quarterly Progress Report of RRBs, 1989.

shows a net addition of 9,346 persons and Rs. 236.49 lakhs of advance between 1984 and 1989. The performance of PGB in this regard is given in Table 5.17. The table shows that financing under the schemes like IRDP and DRI have increased between 1984 and 1989. But with regard to other schemes like ERRP and TRYSEM the performance is not encouraging.

Table 5.17

Schemewise Allocation of Credit by Puri Gramya Bank in 1984 and 1989

(Rs. in Lakhs)

Year	*IRDP*		*DRI*		*OTHERS*		*TOTAL*	
	No. of A/Cs	*Amount*	*No. of A/Cs*	*Amount*	*No. of A/Cs*	*Amount*	*No. of A/Cs*	*Amount*
1984	4241	98.99	2205	53.27	834	13.27	7280	165.53
1989	13327	328.76	3133	67.76	166	5.50	16626	402.02
Net Variation	9086	229.77	928	14.49	-668	-7.77	9346	236.49

Sources: NABARD, Institutional Development Department, RRB Division, *Quarterly Progress Report of RRB*, June 1984 and June 1989.

NABARD

The financial institutions like that of Cooperative Banks, Commercial Banks and Puri Gramya Bank get refinancing accommodation from NABARD to undertake financing of rural artisans and other rural borrowers in the district. It is noticed that the total number of ongoing schemes under implementation in Puri district as on 1988 was 86 in number. Available data further show that upto the same period the NABARD has already refinanced a sum of Rs. 1,108.1 lakhs in the district of Puri. However, It is noticed that the financial institutions have not utilised the refinancing facilities as required.[2]

ORISSA STATE FINANCIAL CORPORATION

Besides all these institutions, Orissa State Financial Corporation is also engaged in financing artisan units functioning in the district. However, the amount of financing is declining in recent years. The table below shows the financing to Village and Cottage Industrial units in the district is declining.

Table 5.18

Financing to Artisan Units by OSFC in Puri District, 1979-80 and 1989-90

(Rs. in Lakhs)

Year	*Accounts (in Nos.)*	*Amount Sanctioned*
1979-80	134	18.72
1988-89	3	1.11
Percentage variation in 1988-89 over 1979-89	(-) 97.8	(-) 94.1

Source: OSFC, Cuttack, Annual Reports, 1979-80 and 1988-89.

The table shows that the financing to the artisan units whereas stood at 18.72 lakhs in 1979-80, the same was only 1.11 lakhs in 1988-89, showing a decrease of 94.1 per cent over the period. Simultaneously, the number of artisans financed has also declined from 134 in 1979-80 to only 3 in 1988-89, showing a decrease in number by 97.8 per cent in the aforesaid period.

Multi Agency Effort in Financing

There has been a multi agency approach to financing rural artisan in the district. The performance of various institutional financing agencies in this regard is given in Table 5.19.

The table shows that the various credit agencies

functioning in the district for financing rural artisans was Rs. 728.43 lakhs in 1989. Of the total financing the share of Co-operative Bank stood at 59.8 per cent. The share of Commercial Banks, Regional Rural Banks and OSFC stood at 24.0, 16.1 and 0.2 per cent respectively in the year referred below.

Table 5.19

Multi Agency Effort in Financing Artisan Units in the District in 1989

Sl. No.	*Institutions*	*Amount financed (in lakhs)*	*% of the total*
1.	Cooperative Banks	435.59	59.8
2.	Commercial Banks	174.73	24.0
3.	Regional Rural Banks	117.00	16.1
4.	Orissa State Financial Corporation	1.11	0.2
	Total	728.43	100.0

Sources: For Sl. No. 1, See Table 5.1 & 5.4
For Sl. No. 2, See Table 5.12.
For Sl. No. 3, See Table 5.16 and
For Sl. No. 4, See Table 5.18.

Relative Performance of Institutional Financing Agencies in the State and at the District

The table below shows that the performance of various financing institutions in the district in relation to that of the state, in matter of financing to rural artisan.

The table shows that financing to artisan units made in the year 1989 in the state stood at 4,801.62 lakhs. This was Rs. 728.43 lakhs at the district level. Percentagewise the share of the district constitute 15.2 to the total credit supplied in the year 1989. Again, of the total financing made by Co-operative Banks in the state, the share of district constitute 16.4 per cent. In case of Commercial Banks,

Regional Rural Banks and OSFC, the relative share stood at 29.2, 7.6 and 22.2 per cent respectively in the aforesaid year. It shows that Commercial Bank's have played an important role in financing rural artisans compared to other agencies.

Table 5.20

Relative Performance of Institutional Agencies in the State and at the District

(Rs. in lakhs)

Sl. No.	*Institutions*	*Amount advanced in the state*	*Amount advanced in the district*	*% share of district to the state total*
1.	Cooperative Banks	2658.59	435.59	16.4
2.	Commercial Banks	598.00	174.73	29.2
3.	Regional Rural Banks	1540.04	117.00	7.6
4.	Orissa State Financial Corporation	4.99	1.11	22.2
	Total	4801.62	728.43	15.2

Sources: (1) See Chapter IV, Table 4.21
(2) See Chapter V, Table 5.19

REFERENCES

1. UCO Bank, Lead Bank Office, *Annual Action Plan for Puri*, (1988-89).

2. *Ibid.*

6

Demand for and Supply of Credit: The Credit Gap

Right from the beginning of the bank nationalisation in the year 1969, the institutional agencies have shouldered the responsibility of financing the rural artisans in the state, as well as in the district. Their vast branch network and the system of operation have been tailor made for the purpose of solving the institutional credit needs of the hitherto neglected sectors, including rural artisans. It is observed from the foregoing chapters that in spite of the massive expansion and operation of institutional credit agencies the supply of credit to rural artisans has not increased significantly over the years.

As against this, the credit needs and requirements of the rural artisans have undergone a significant change in recent years. More particularly due to rapid expansion of bank branches in the remote rural areas, liberalisation of loan policy and credit procedures and implementation of various poverty alleviation schemes by Government etc. have helped to arouse the needs and requirements of rural artisans. Consequently, the demand for credit by the rural artisans has gone up considerably in the recent years. Furthermore, the rural artisans who were mostly satisfying their credit needs, through non-institutional financing agencies before are interested, at present, to avail their increasing credit requirements from institutional financing agencies to a greater extent.

Against this background an attempt is made in this chapter to discuss about the demand for and supply of credit by the institutional credit agencies. There is also an attempt to study the possible credit gap that may exist on account of the mis-match between the demand for and supply of credit. Furthermore, an attempt is also made to discuss about the pattern of utilisation of the credit received from the institutional sources by the sample artisans and to reveal the utilisation gap, that exist if any.

It is noticed that the rural artisans need credit for various purposes. They require working capital, term capital and consumption loans to pursue their economic activities. Working capital is required to pursue their day to day industrial operations. The term capital is required by the artisans for buying machines, tools and equipments. It is also required for adopting new technology and improved techniques of production etc. Apart from this the artisans also require loans for consumption purposes during the actual process of work. Such loans help the rural artisans to sustain themselves during the period when they are actually engaged in production activities.

In general, amount of credit required by rural artisans was estimated by a committee headed by W.S. Tambey. The committee was appointed by Government of India. According to the committee, "Artisans (irrespective of location) of units engaged in small industrial activities (manufacturing, processing and preservation and servicing in villages and small towns with a population not exceeding 50,000 involving utilisation of locally available natural resources and/or human skills are eligible for loan from banks on specially, favourable terms." The maximum total credit requirement of an industrial artisan engaged in village or a cottage unit is put by the committee at Rs. 25,000. Credit upto this amount includes both working capital and term capital. Besides, the institutional financing agencies are also required to sanction credit for consumption purposes, which the artisans need at the time of actual involvement in the work.[1] Besides the recommendation of Tambey Committee the total composite credit requirement of an artisan unit is fixed upto Rs. 30 thousands by NABARD Artisan units living in rural and semi urban areas can avail loan facility upto Rs. 30 thousands under the refinancing scheme of NABARD, through various institutional financing agencies, like Co-operative Banks, Commercial Banks and Regional Rural Banks[2]. The amount of Rs. 30 thousand cover both the working capital as well as block capital needs of the artisans. It may be observed that the above credit requirement is fixed without any margin money, requirement.

Moreover, credit requirement by artisan borrowers coming under the normal category and under schemes are also fixed separately. It is noticed that artisans are mostly financed either under normal category or under schemes like IRDP, ERRP and NREP etc. The Lead Bank of the district in consultation with other institutional agencies has also made certain general suggestions about fixing the unit cost or credit requirement of various artisans in general. It has suggested that artisan units which are being financed under normal category or without under any scheme may be financed upto an amount of Rs. 4,500. And if they are financed under any scheme having subsidy component, they will be financed upto an amount of Rs. 3,000. Besides, credit requirement of an artisan unit coming under the ISB (Industry Service and Business) component of IRDP scheme have also been prefixed by the institutional financing agencies at Rs. 10 thousand.[3]

However, it is true that the unit cost prescribed for a particular type of unit will not be applicable for all the artisan units coming under the same category. Though the rural artisans mostly live in rural area yet their housing conditions, family compositions, quality of product, occupational status, experience and skill etc. vary from each other. Hence the credit limit for each of the artisan based units as per the above criterion may not be suitable.

Over the years various committees have been formed

and they have prescribed various yardsticks to estimate the credit needs of artisan borrowers. Accordingly credit limit fixed at Rs. 25 thousands per artisan based unit appear to be more plausible. It is further recommended that the institutional financing agencies will not insist on collateral security for sanctioning credit upto the prescribed credit limit of Rs. 25,000. The objective behind this policy is that, no worthwhile credit proposals need be turned down, for want of collateral securities or guarantees. Besides, it was further envisaged that 60 to 80 per cent of the credit requirements by the artisans would be dispensed by the Branch Manager at the branch level itself. The intention is that the credit limits of Rs. 25,000 should be disposed of within a period of four weeks from the date of receipt of the applicationform from the artisan borrower.

It is noticed that commercial banks and other financial institutions, mostly adopt interview-cum-appraisal method while making an estimation about the credit needs of rural artisans. By this method both the term capital as well as working capital needs of an artisan unit are estimated.[4] It is further noticed that the institutional financing agencies while estimating the demand for credit in relation to working capital needs, mostly take the 'lead time' into consideration. The lead time is thus required to determine the number of production cycles in a particular artisan industrial unit. Production cycle is generally termed as operation cycle. A manufacturing unit is generally observed to be governed by a cycle of operation. The cycle constitutes a period in which the cash is converted into raw materials and raw materials into finished products and realisation of cash by sale of finished goods. The operation cycle thus is a time, that elapses between cash outlay and cash realisation by the sales of finished goods and the realisation of sundry debtors. The cycle thus comprises the components like (a) lead time for acquiring raw materials and coverage period for which they are in store, (b) conversion or process time, (c) average period for which the finished goods are in store, and (d) the average collection period of receivables. The artisan units require separate time for these various purposes and adding together all the time required for various purposes in total, the number of operation cycles in a particular year can be calculated very well. The operating cycle method, as stated above, is accepted at the banking circle, as the most important and suitable method for estimating credit needs of artisan units coming for loan of Rs. 25 thousand.

In case an artisan puts forward a demand for term capital then in the banking circle it is generally estimated according to simple interview method. However, in this context banks generally utilise their own knowledge about the village, person and the project to be undertaken. But it was noticed that artisans put forward a credit need for consumption purposes besides working capital and term capital needs. According to the instructions given to financial institutions by the RBI, the composite loan to artisans and village and cottage industries may include a component to meet the essential consumption needs of the borrowers. However, the amount in no case exceed Rs. 500, per artisan. According to the yardstick, in the process of estimating the credit needs of sample artisan units, the consumption needs of artisans are also duly taken into consideration.

Demand for Credit

The credit requirement of the sample artisans is estimated according to the usual procedure as stated above by the financial institutions. The demand for credit is thus estimate in relation to industrial activities of the unit, for the year preceding the actual receipt of assistance. The credit requirement is estimated in relation to sample artisans numbering 120 and belonging to 10 artisan units. This is shown in Table 6.1.

The total requirement of credit in relation to all the sample artisans are estimated to be Rs. 6.98 lakhs. Of this credit requirement, working capital, term capital and consumption credit account for 81.7, 9.5, 8.8 per cent respectively. It reveals that rural artisans mostly require credit to meet working capital needs to meet their day to day expenses in the operation of the industrial units. The table reveals that the demand for term capital is not significant enough. It accounts for less than 10 per cent of the total capital needs. Besides term capital and working capital, artisans also require consumption credit to sustain themselves in the process of their industrial activities.

Table 6.1

Purposewise and Craftwise Distribution of Demand for Credit, 1987

(in Rupees)

Category of Artisans	*Total credit needs*	*Working capital needs*	*Term capital needs*	*Consumption loan*
1. Pottery	124750 (100.0)	99800 (80.0)	8000 (6.4)	16950 (13.6)
2. Bamboo Work	24000 (100.0)	19000 (79.2)	– (20.8)	5000
3. Weaving	65000 (100.0)	45000 (69.2)	12000 (18.5)	8000 (12.3)
4. Bell Metal	227500 (100.0)	190000 (83.5)	27500 (12.1)	10000 (4.4)
5. Stone Carving	40000 (100.0)	30000 (75.0)	9000 (22.5)	1000 (2.5)
6. Applique	120000 (100.0)	104000 (86.7)	10000 (8.3)	6000 (5.0)
7. Pattachitra	18000 (100.0)	15400 (85.5)	–	26000 (14.5)
8. Papier Mache	30500 (100.0)	27500 (88.3)	–	3000 (11.5)
9. Beads Making	30000 (100.0)	25000 (83.3)	–	5000 (16.7)
10 Coir Works	18000 (100.0)	15000 (83.3)	–	3000 (16.7)
Total	697750 (100.0)	570700 (81.7)	66500 (9.5)	61050 (8.8)

Source : Data compiled from the field study (1989).

N.B. : Estimation of the demand for credit is made on the basis of Operation Cycle Method.

An analysis of artisan unit-wise demand for working capital needs reveal that units accounting for 80 percent and more than 80 per cent of working capital needs are pottery, bell metal, applique, pattachitra, papier machie, beads making and coir works etc. These units account for 80.0, 83.5, 86.7, 85.5, 88.3, 83.3 and 83.3 per cents respectively of the total credit requirement. This is observed in Table 5.1.

As against this working capital needs of the artisan units like Bamboo works, Weaving, Stone carving, account for 79, 69 and 75 per cents respectively of their total credit requirement. On the whole, it may be observed that almost all the artisan based units need larger amount of working capital for the operation of the units.

Field study shows that some of the sample artisans engaged in trades like pottery, weaving, bell metal, and stone carving and applique etc. also needed term capital for their units. The term capital requirement out of the total estimated credit need was 6.4, 18.5, 12.1, 22.5 and 8.3 per cents respectively. However, it is noticed that, stone carving artisans generally need more term loans for the purpose of constructing storage facilities for safe keeping of statutes and images and for expanding the working space in their own houses. As against these, artisans engaged in the trades like, bamboo basket making, pattachitra, papier machie, beads making and coir works do not requires any credit towards meeting block capital. It is due to the fact that these units require tools and equipments which are simple, low cost and indigenous in nature. And again the trades are of such type that once fixed investment is made for acquiring tools and implements, no further investment is required for quite a long period of time for acquiring these items.

Besides, working capital and term capital requirements, almost all sample artisan units require credit for consumption purpose. The units do not provide employment to the artisans for the whole of the year. This happens due to non-availability of raw materials and slackening of demand for the products by the consumers etc. So to sustain themselves in trade and their family, they require consumption loans. According to the yardstick adopted by the financial institutions the credit requirement for consumption purposes is fixed between Rs. 250 and Rs. 500 per individual artisan. On the basis of this the demand for credit by the sample artisans was estimated and shown. Table 5.1 referred to earlier shows that, of the total credit required by the artisans consumption loan constitute nearly 8.8 per cent. The table shows that in case of seven out of ten types of artisan units the consumption need varies between 10 per cent and 20 per cent of the total requirement. It is only in case of three out of 10 types of units that percentage distribution of consumption credit out of the total is less than 10 per cent.

Purposewise Credit Requirements

The field study reveals that the artisans require a higher dose of working capital for the purpose of purchasing raw materials. It is observed that the sample artisans required nearly 54.0 per cent of total credit for the purpose of procuring raw materials. Another 18.8 per cent of the total credit need they required for payment of wages. Thus, 72.8 per cent of total credit requirements, the sample artisans need for the purpose of procuring raw material and for the payment of wages. This is seen from Table 6.2 . Credit required out of the total for payment of rent, interest, transport charges, electricity dues and miscellaneous expenses etc. account for only 8.9 per cent. The total working capital need out of the total credit requirement stands at 81.7 per cent.

So far as the term capital requirement is concerned it is noticed from the table that the sample artisans mainly required such credit for purposes like; construction of factory sheds, purchase of machines and for construction of storage facilities. For all these purposes, they need 9.5 per cent of total credit requirement. It is further evident that for consumption purposes, the sample artisans need 8.8 per cent of total credit requirement. This will help them to engage themselves in the process of actual production activities.

Table 6.2

Purposewise Distribution of Demand for Credit (1987)

(in Rupees)

Purpose of credit required	*Amount of loan required*	*Percent to the grand total*
I. Working Capital		
(a) Raw materials	3,76,662	54.0
(b) Payment of wages	1,31,261	18.8
(c) Payment of rent	5,707	0.9
(d) Payment of interest	22,828	3.2
(e) Payment of transport charges	11,414	1.6
(f) Payment of Electricity dues	22,828	3.2
Total (a to f)	5,70,700	81.7
II Term Capital		
(a) Constructing factory shed	14,630	2.1
(b) Machines & Tools	19,285	2.8
(c) Expansion, innovation and modernisation	15,960	2.3
(d) For shortage & godown	16,625	2.4
Total (a+b+c+d)	66,500	9.5
III Consumption Loan	61,050	8.8
Total (I+II+III)	6,97,750	100.0

Source: Data compiled from the field study, 1989.

Per Capita Credit Requirement

The Table 6.3 reveals about the per capita credit requirement of the sample artisans. It is noticed that the per capita demand for credit of all the sample artisans in general stood at about Rs. 5,815 in the year under study. It is further noticed that the per capita credit requirement is varying between Rs. 2,407 and Rs. 10,000 per artisan. It is further noticed that the unit cost of artisan units is very much low in most of the cases. The Table 6.3 shows that, in case of 56 sample artisan units, or 46.6 per cent of the total artisans studied the unit cost is limited between Rs. 2,400 and 4,500. The sample artisan units coming under the category mentioned above are bamboo basket makers, weavers, beads makers, coir workers and artisans engaged in pattachitra etc. These units are having per capita credit requirement at Rs. 2,667, Rs. 2,407, Rs. 3,000, Rs. 3,000 and Rs. 4,500, respectively in the reference year.

Table 6.3

Per Capita Demand for Credit (1987)

(in Rupees)

	Category of Artisans	*No. of Artisans studied*	*% of the total*	*Total demand for credit*	*Per capita demand for credit*
1.	Pottery	17	14.2	1,24,750	7,338
2.	Bamboo Work	9	7.5	24,000	2,667
3.	Weaving	27	22.5	65,000	2,407
4.	Bell Metal	25	20.8	2,27,500	9,100
5.	Stone Carving	4	3.3	40,000	10,000
6.	Applique	12	10.0	1,20,000	10,000
7.	Patta Chitra	4	3.3	18,000	4,500
8.	Papier Machie	6	5.0	30,500	5,083
9.	Beads Making	10	8.3	30,000	3,000
10	Coir Works	6	5.0	18,000	3,000
	Total	120	100.0	6,97,750	5,814.5

Source: Data compiled from the field study, 1989.

However rest 64 number of sample artisans engaged in trades like, stone carving, applique, bell metal works, pottery, and papier machie require per capita credit upto Rs. 10,000 Rs. 10,000 Rs. 9,100 Rs. 7,338 and Rs. 5,083 respectively in the reference year. These units need more per capita credit due to the reason that their scale of operation is seen to be bigger than that of the other artisan units. Besides the products manufactured by them are also observed to be mostly of durable and lasting in nature.

The average per capita demand for credit for 120 sample artisans selected for the study, as revealed from the table, stands at about Rs. 5,815. This is somewhat higher than the per capita demand for credit of Rs. 4,500 as suggested by District Credit Plan, Puri for artisan units. The increased higher average per capita demand for credit is primarily due to higher rise in costs.

Supply of Credit

To meet the demand for credit of the sample artisans the institutional financing agencies are the most important source of supply of finance. In recent years, there is massive growth in the number of institutional financing agencies in the state as well as in the district. So, it becomes easier for the rural artisans to get the credit as required.

It is noticed that the sample artisans mostly have procured credit from Cooperative Banks, Commercial Banks and Puri Gramya Bank. As a matter of fact, they have not received any credit from Orissa State Financial Corporation. Probably the sample artisans have not approached OSFC for loan purpose.

Prior to nationalisation the credit requirement of the artisans units was met mostly by non institutional agencies. After nationalisation, on account of the spread of banking facilities in the rural areas the importance of institutional credit agencies have increased considerably. Inspite of this, influence of non-institutional sources in supplying credit to artisans has not been totally eliminated. They are still active and help the rural artisans by supplying finance on easier

Table 6.4

Supply of Credit to Sample Artisans by Institutional and Non-Institutional Sources, 1987

(Amount in Rupees)

Sources	*Amount of Loan Supplied*							
	Total loan supplied	*% to the total*	*Short term loan*	*% to the total*	*Long term loan*	*% to the total*	*Consum-ption*	*% to the total*
I. Institutional :								
(a) Co-operative Bank	103,750	22.4	95,750 (92.3)	21.3	8,000 (7.7)	49.7	–	–
(b) Commercial Bank	113,400 (100.0)	24.5	1,07,430 (95.4)	23.9	5,970 (4.6)	29.6	–	–
(c) Regional Rural Bank	200,600 (100.0)	43.3	1,94,400 (86.9)	42.4	6,200 (3.1)	30.7	–	–
Total	417,750 (100.0)	90.1	3,97,580 (95.2)	92.0	20,170 (4.8)	100.0	–	–

(Contd.)

II. Non-Institutional :								
(a) Money Lenders	26,000 (100.0)	5.6	20,000 (76.9)	4.4	–	–	6,000 (23.1)	54.5
(b) Friends and Relatives	20,000 (100.0)	4.3	15,000 (75.0)	3.3	–	–	5,000 (25.0)	45.5
Total	46,000 (100.0)	9.9	35,000 (76.0)	7.8	–	–	11,000 (24.0)	100.0
Total : (I + II)	463,750 (100.0)	100.0	4,32,580 (93.0)	100.0	20,170 (4.3)	100.0	11,000 (2.4)	100.0

Source: As per data compiled from the field study and institutional financing agencies.
N. B. : Figures in brackets indicate percent to the total. * Year under consideration, Jan. to Dec.

terms. But in course of their operation they exploit the rural artisans by charging exorbitant rate of interest. The supply of credit to the sample artisans from different sources; institutional and non-institutional is shown in Table 5.4.

The Table 6.4 shows that the sample artisans have availed nearly a total amount of Rs. 4.64 lakhs loan from both institutional and non-institutional sources. It is observed that while the institutional agencies accounted for about 90 per cent of the total supply of credit, the non institutional agencies accounted for only 10 per cent of the total. This clearly indicates that the important of non-institutional agencies in the field of supply of credit has considerably reduced though not totally eliminated. On the other hand, institutional agencies are instrumental in supplying a sizeable amount of credit to sample artisans in the district. As mentioned earlier the All India Debt Investment Survey conducted by R.B.I. in the year 1971 revealed that the non institutional agencies whereas accounted for 92.6 per cent of total supply of credit, the institutional agencies accounted for only 7.4 per cent of the total. But it is revealing to note that in the recent years the situation has been reversed. This healthy development has contributed substantially for solving the financial problems of rural artisans.

Table 6.4 further reveals that the sample rural artisans have received the entire non-institutional credit towards meeting the working capital needs, and not toward term capital requirement. It is further observed from the field study that artisans mostly belonging to the category of applique and bell metal craft and Beads making etc. at times meet their working capital requirement through the non institutional sources like money lenders and etc. They accept these type of financing due to the fact that the borrowing from these sources is available without too much formalities, and easily. Sometimes, the artisan units received orders from agencies belonging to the category of non-institutional sources. For this the agencies mainly supply credit in advance to the borrowers with the condition that their products need be sold only through them. So, being unable to get financing from institutional sources readily, they move to non institutional sources which supply bulk of the working capital requirement and carry out their production activities.

It may be observed from the table that out of the total loan supplied to the rural artisans units, Rs. 1.04 lakhs, Rs. 1.13 lakhs and Rs. 2.01 lakhs have been supplied by Co-operative Banks, Commercial Banks, and Puri Gramya Bank respectively. In terms of percentage, the proportion of credit supplied by Co-operative Banks, Commercial Banks, and RRB/Puri Gramya Bank to the total credit deployed was 22.4, 24.5 and 43.3 per cent respectively in the reference year. This clearly indicates that out of the institutional financing agencies RRB/Puri Gramya Bank has deployed a larger amount of credit for the benefit of rural artisans.

It is evident from the Table 6.4 that the institutional credit agencies have deployed nearly 85.7 per cent of the total credit by all sources towards working capital needs. As against this, in case of term capital it is only 4.3 per cent. The balance amount was supplied by non-institutional sources in the form of working and block capital. It shows that the institutional financing agencies have supplied a greater percentage share of loan towards meeting working capital requirement. The share of loan towards term capital stood at a low level. It is revealed from the foregoing table that the institutional credit agencies have not undertaken the supply of consumption loan to sample artisans, although they are categorically required to provide the same. Whatever consumption loan was supplied to sample artisans they were dispensed by non-institutional agencies.

Craftwise and Institutional Sourcewise Distribution of Credit to Sample Artisans

The Table 6.5 shows that the total sample artisans numbering 120, have received a total amount of Rs. 4.18 lakhs from institutional sources. Percentagewise, the Cooperative Bank account for 24.8 and Commercial Banks

Table 6.5

Categorywise and Institutional Sourcewise Distribution of Credit to Sample Artisans (1987)

Category of Artisan Craft	*No. of sample artisans studied*	*Co-operative Bank / Co-op. Soc.*		*Commercial Bank*		*R R B*		*Total amount financed*	*% to the total*
		Amount	*% to the total*	*Amount*	*% to the total*	*Amount*	*% to the total*		
1. Pottery	17	1,03,750 (83.1)	100.0	–	–	21,000 (16.9)	10.5	1,24,750	29.9
2. Bamboo Works	9	–	–	6,900 (100.0)	6.1	–	–	6,900 (100.0)	1.7
3. Weaving	27	–	–	–	–	25,000 (100.0)	12.5	25,000 (100.0)	6.0
4. Bell Metal	25	–	–	12,000 (12.1)	10.5	87,000 (87.9)	44.0	99,000 (100.0)	23.7
5. Stone Carving	4	–	–	34,000 (100.0)	30.0	–	–	34,000 (100.0)	8.1
6. Applique	12	–	–	60,500 (84.6)	53.4	11,000 (15.4)	5.5	71,500 (100.0)	17.1

(Contd.)

7. Pattrachitra	4	–	–	–	–	8,900 (100.0)	4.5	8,900 (100.0)	2.1
8. Papier Machie	6	–	–	–	–	18,600 (100.0)	9.8	18,600 (100.0)	4.5
9. Beads Making	10	–	–	–	–	20,700 (100.0)	10.4	20,700 (100.0)	5.0
10 Coir Works	6	–	–	–	–	8,400 (100.0)	3.9	8,400 (100.0)	2.0
Total	120	1,03,750 (24.8)	100.0	1,13,400 (27.2)	100.0	2,00,600 (48.0)	100.0	4,17,750 (100.0)	100.00

Source: Data compiled as per filed study and from institutional financing agencies.
N. B. : Figures in brackets indicate percent to the total.
Year under consideration, Jan. to Dec.

account for 27.2 per cent of the total finance deployed to sample artisans from institutional sources. It is revealing to note that Puri Gramya Bank has supplied a major portion i.e. 48.0 per cent of the total financing to sample artisans.

Craftwise, the table further reveals that the percentage distribution of credit, out of the total finance deployed to 120 sample artisans by all institutional agencies stood at 29.9 per cent in case of pottery artisans units. Next to pottery artisan units, Bell metal artisan units, applique artisans units and stone carving units accounted for 23.7 per cent, 17.1 per cent and 8.1 per cent respectively of the total finance deployed by institutional agencies to all craft units studied in the district. It may be observed that except the pottery units, who have received bulk of the finance from Co-operative, no other artisan craft units have received any amount of finance from this institution. Bulk of the artisan units have received credit mainly from Commercial Banks and Puri Gramya Bank, who together accounted for 75.2 per cent of the total credit dispensed by the institutional agencies to sample artisans. Supply of finance by Puri Gramya Bank accounts for the largest proportion out of the total, and it is made available to sample artisans both normally and under various schemes like IRDP, ERRP and DIR etc.

It may further be observed that although the Co-operatives supply finance to pottery units, yet they also undertake the responsibility of supplying raw materials under production-cum-sale basis to weaving and bell metal units with the condition that the finished products will only be sold through the Co-operatives. But it is explicitly clear that bulk of the selected sample artisans procure funds mainly from Commercial Banks and Puri Gramya Bank.

Craftwise and Purposewise Distribution of Credit

Purposewise distribution of institutional credit to the sample artisans shows that most of the credit is supplied in the form of working capital. Table 6.6 shows the purposewise distribution of institutional finances to different category of artisans.

Table 6.6

Purposewise and Craftwise Distribution of Credit Supplied by Institutional Financing Agencies to Sample Artisans, 1987*

(in Rupees)

Category of Artisan	*No. of Artisans*	*Short-term loan*	*Term loan*	*Cons-umption loan*	*Total*
1. Pottery	17 (14.1)	1,16,750 (93.8)	8,000 (6.2)	–	1,24,750 (100.0)
2. Bamboo Work	9 (7.5)	6,900 (100.0)	–	–	6,900 (100.0)
3. Weaving	25 (20.8)	20,000 (80.0)	5,000 (20.0)	–	25,000 (100.0)
4. Bell Metal	27 (22.5)	99,000 (100.0)	–	–	99,000 (100.0)
5. Stone Carving	4 (3.3)	34,000 (100.0)	–	–	34,000 (100.0)
6. Applique	12 (10.0)	65,530 (91.7)	5,970 (8.3)	–	71,500 (100.0)
7. Patta Chitra	4 (3.3)	8,900 (100.0)	–	–	8,900 (100.0)
8. Papier Machie	6 (5.0)	18,000 (96.8)	600 (3.2)	–	18,600 (100.0)
9. Beads Making	10 (8.3)	20,700 (100.0)	–	–	20,700 (100.0)
10 Coir Works	6 (5.0)	7,800 (83.0)	600 (7.0)	–	8,400 (100.0)
Total	120 (100.0)	3,97,580 (95.2)	20,170 (4.8)	–	4,17,750 (100.0)

Source: Data compiled from field study .

* Year under consideration – January to December.

N.B. : Figures in bracket indicate percentage to the total.

Table 6.6 shows that out of the total loan supplied to the sample artisans, 95.2 per cent are supplied in the form of working capital needs and 4.8 per cent are supplied towards meeting block capital requirement by institutional financing agencies. The institutions have mainly supplied funds in the shape of working capital to the artisans engaged in the trades like bamboo works, bell metal works, stone carving units, pattachitra units and beads making units. As against this, artisans engaged in pottery, weaving, and applique units have received more than 80 per cent of their need in the form of working capital and the balance in the form of term capital. It may be observed that institutional credit agencies have not supplied any credit to sample artisans in the form of consumption loans.

Per Capita Credit Supplied

It is noticed that the average per capita credit supplied to the sample artisans stood at Rs. 3,481 in the year under reference. This is shown in Table 6.7. The Table 6.7 further clearly shows that the per capita credit supplied to sample artisans mostly vary between Rs. 766 and Rs. 8,500. It is noticed that whereas the artisans like bamboo basket makers and weavers are mostly coming under the lowest category, artisans in stone carving, pottery and applique units are coming under the higher category.

The table further shows that about 35.8 per cent of artisans studied are having a per capita loan amount of less than Rs. 1,500, 18.3 per cent of artisans are having a per capita supply of credit between Rs. 3,001 and Rs. 5,000, an 27.5 per cent of artisans studied are being supplied with a per capita loan of Rs. 5,000 and above. It reveals that nearly 56 per cent of the sample artisans are provided with a per capita loan assistance of Rs. 3,000 only. This indicates that a larger percentage of artisans have received a low amount of assistance from the existing institutional financing agencies. It is further seen from the table that there is a substantial mismatch between demand for and supply of credit amongst the sample artisans. The analysis of this can be observed from the following paragraphs.

Credit Gap

The Table 6.7 also shows the gap between credit required by the artisans borrowers and credit supplied to them by institutional financing agencies. It is noticed that the artisans required a total credit of Rs. 6.98 lakhs to satisfy their credit needs. However, the institutional agencies supplied only Rs. 4.18 lakhs to the artisans to meet the credit requirement. As a result there is the gap of Rs. 2.80 lakhs in the year under reference. This indicates that the demand for credit was more, whereas the supply of credit was inadequate to meet the demand. Percentage gap to the total credit demanded was 40.1 per cent in the year under consideration.

Looking at artisan unitwise credit gap, the available data as shown in Table 6.7 reveal that the credit gap varies between Rs. 6 thousand and 1.28 lakhs. In percentage term artisan units having more than 50 per cent of credit gap are bamboo basket making unit, weaving, bell metal, pattachitra and coir works. Artisan units having credit gap varying between 30 per cent and 50 per cent are : Applique units, papier machie and Beads making. The only unit where the credit gap is less than 20 per cent is stone carving. It may, however, be observed that the pottery units have not faced any credit gap. In the case of pottery unit, there is a balance between demand for and supply of credit thus leaving no credit gap.

Looking at per capita credit gap, it is observed from the table that the average credit gap for the artisans stood at Rs. 2,333 in the year under reference. It is noticed that, whereas the per capita credit demand stood at Rs. 5,814.5 per capita credit supply stood at Rs. 3,481.2 thus leaving a credit gap of Rs. 2,333.3 in the year under reference. An analysis of artisan craftwise credit gap reveals that the pottery artisans do not have any credit gap. However, it is

Table 6.7

Demand for and Supply of Credit* and the Credit Gap (1986-87)

(in Rupees)

CATEGORY OF ARTISANS	No. artisans unit studied	Total credit required	Total credit supplied**	Gap in Rupees	% gap	Per capita credit required	Per capita credit supplied	Per capita credit gap in Rs.
1. Pottery	17 (14.1)	1,24,750	1,24,750	–	–	7,338	7,338	–
2. Bamboo Works	9 (7.5)	24,000	6,900	17,100	71.3	2,667	766	1,901
3. Weaving	27 (20.8)	65,000	25,000	40,000	61.5	2,407	926	1,481
4. Bell Metal	25 (22.5)	2,27,500	99,000	1,28,500	56.5	9,100	3,900	5,140
5. Stone Carving	4 (3.3)	40,000	34,000	6,000	15.0	10,000	8,500	1,500
6. Applique	12 (10.0)	1,20,000	71,500	48,500	40.4	10,000	5,958	4,042
7. Pattrachitra	4 (3.3)	18,000	8,900	9,100	50.6	4,500	2,225	2,275
8. Papier Machie	6 (5.0)	30,500	18,600	11,900	39.0	5,083	3,100	1,983
9. Beads Making	10 (8.3)	30,000	20,700	9,300	31.0	3,000	2,070	930
10 Coir Works	6 (5.0)	18,000	8,400	9,600	53.3	3,000	1,400	1,600
Total	120 (100.0)	6,97,750	4,17,750	2,80,000	40.1	5,814.5	3,481.2	2,333.3

Source: Data compiled as per sample study.

* Refers to only institutional credit, ** 1987 year under consideration from January to December. Figures in brackets indicate percentage to the credit required.

noticed that the greater amount of credit gap is noticed in the case of Bell metal artisans, which stood at Rs. 5,140. Next to bell metal artisans are the applique artisans who had a credit gap of Rs. 4,042. The lowest amount of credit gap is visualized in the case of Beads making artisans. It stood at Rs. 930 in the reference year.

It may be observed that almost all the artisans except the pottery artisans, experienced a sizeable amount of credit gap. For this most of these artisans primarily depended upon sources other than institutional financing agencies. Often they also depended upon their own resources to bridge the gap. The artisans in course of their industrial operation have tried to meet the credit gap from non institutional sources. It was noticed that of the total credit gap of Rs. 2.80 lakhs in the references year, the non-institutional agencies met a sum of Rs. 46,000 to bridge the gap (Table 6.4). Percentagewise, this accounts for 16.4 of the total credit gap. The balance 83.6 of the credit gap was not met from any other sources. It is noteworthy to mention that the artisans facing a credit gap did not like to borrow from non-institutional sources, due to higher rate of interest charged by them.

Credit gap can also be discussed by taking the general unit cost of these artisan units as prescribed by the Annual Action Plan specifically prescribed for the district. As mentioned earlier the unit cost of these units under normal category and under a scheme was fixed at Rs. 4,500 and Rs. 3,000 respectively. If for instance, the unit cost of required credit need of all the sleeted sample artisan units is put under normal category the estimated required credit amount comes to be Rs. 5.40 lakhs. According to the present study, the credit actually received stood at Rs. 4.18 lakhs. In terms of percentage, the credit gap thus comes to Rs. 22.6 per cent of the total credit required.

Thus, it is noticed that there has been inadequate supply of institutional financing to the artisans over all these years in the state as well as in the district. As a result of which there exist a significant gap between the demand for credit and the supply of credit disbursed to them. Thus the artisan units are being underfinanced by the institutional financing agencies.

Utilisation of Credit

But to add to the problem more, it is also observed that the artisans have not utilised the loan properly whatever they have received from the institutional financing agencies. As stated earlier, the institutional financing agencies have not supplied any consumption credit to the sample artisans in the district. Consequently there has taken place some misutilisation of fund from one purpose to the other purpose and for plain consumption. The main objective of institutional financing agencies is to ensure proper utilisation of loans advanced by them to artisans. Once the scheme is approved and the loan is sanctioned on the basis of the schemes, the institutional financing agencies thereafter undertake the responsibility of conducting follow up action and supervision to assess the enduse of credit.

However, due to inadequate supply of finance compared to growing demand for credit, artisan borrowers after receiving the loan face certain difficulties in procuring complementary inputs for the implementation of the project. Besides, it is often noticed that although the fund is sanctioned for one purpose, yet it is found to be utilized for other purposes. This has resulted in utilization gap. This is shown in Table 6.8.

The table shows the purposewise utilisation of credit and the gap in utilisation of loans sanctioned to artisan borrowers. It is observed that the institutional financing agencies have supplied a total amount of Rs. 4.18 lakhs to 120 sample selected artisans belonging to different crafts in the year under consideration. After receiving the loan, the artisan borrowers have utilised a total sum of Rs. 3.49 lakhs. It means 83.5 per cent of the total loan sanctioned has been utilised by the sample artisans. This indicates that there is a gap of Rs. 0.69 lakhs arising out of the difference between total supply of credit and total utilisation of credit. Percentagewise this accounts for 16.5 per cent of the total supply of credit.

Table 6.8

Purposewise Utilisation of Loan and the Utilisation Gap

(in Rupees)

Purpose	Supply of credit	Utilisation of credit	Utilisation gap (in Rs.)	Gap in terms of % to be the total credit supplied
1. Working Capital	3,97,580 (95.2)	2,16,950 (61.0)	1,80,630	45.4
2. Term Capital	20,170 (4.8)	20,170 (4.6)	–	–
3. Consumption Loans	–	1,12,050 (34.7)	1,12,050	100.0
Total	4,17,750 (100.0)	3,49,170 (100.0)	68,580	16.5

Source : Data compiled from the field study 1989.
Figures in parentheses indicate percentage to the total.

It is further observed that the institutional financing agencies have supplied Rs. 3.98 lakhs for working capital purposes. For term capital they supplied 0.20 lakhs. Percentagewise the ratio of working capital and term capital to total supply of credit stood at 95.2 per cent and 4.8 per cent. It is observed that of the total amount supplied for working capital, only 61.0 per cent was utilized for working capital purposes by artisan borrowers. So far as term capital is concerned, the amount was fully utilised by the artisan borrowers for the purpose for which it was supplied.

However, it is noticed from the available data that the institutional financing agencies had not supplied any credit to artisan borrowers towards consumption requirement. On the other hand, it is noticed that the artisan borrowers had utilized a sum of Rs. 1.12 lakhs for meeting consumption needs. The unutilised amount from working capital source had been utilised for meeting consumption needs. There is unutilised working capital amount of Rs. 1.81 lakhs and of this an amount of Rs. 1.12 lakhs was diverted and utilised for consumption purposes. Percentagewise, of the total unutilised working capital amount, 62 cent was utilised for consumption needs. The balance of 0.69 lakhs or 38 per cent of the total unutilised working capital fund was used for purposes other than for which it was sanctioned.

Craftwise Utilisation Gap

Table 6.9 reveals the craftwise utilisation of loan by sample artisans. It reveals that artisans engaged in trades like; stone carving, applique, pattachitra and papier machie are observed to have utilised the entire credit they have received either for working capital or for term capital or for consumption purposes. Of the total loan advanced to the stone carving sample artisans, they have utilised 88.2 per cent and 11.8 per cent of the loan for working capital purposes and consumption purposes respectively. In the same manner, the applique artisans have utilised 74.9 per cent 8.4 per cent and 16.7 per cent for working capital, term capital and consumption need respectively. Like wise the artisans engaged in Pattachitra and Papier machie have also utilised 84.7 per cent and 59.1 per cent respectively of the total financing towards working capital needs. The percentage share of loan utilised for consumption purposes stood at 15.3 and 37.6 per cent of the total supply of capital respectively. It shows that the above mentioned units have utilised the entire loan received for industrial purposes. But they have not utilised the fund received exactly for the purpose for which it was supplied. As for example, although the stone carving artisans have received the entire loan for working capital purposes yet they have utilised 88.2 per cent for working capital purpose and the balance 11.8 per cent

Table 6.9

Purposewise and Craftwise Utilisation of Credit

(in Rupees)

CATEGORY OF ARTISANS	Supply of Credit				Utilisation of Credit				Utilisation of Gap			
	Short-term loan	Long term loan	Consumption loan	Total	Short-term purposes	Long-term purposes	Consumption purposes	Total	Short-term purposes	Long-term purposes	Consumption purposes	Total gap
1. Pottery	1,16,750 (93.8)	8,000 (6.2)	–	1,24,750 (100.0)	39,920 (32.0)	8,000 (6.4)	40,800 (32.7)	88,720 (71.1)	76,830	Nil	40,800	36,030 (28.9)
2. Bamboo Works	6,900 (100.0)	–	–	6,900 (100.0)	2,250 (32.6)	–	2,650 (38.4)	4,900 (71.0)	4,650	–	2,650	2,000 (29.0)
3. Weaving	20,000 (80.0)	5,000 (20.0)	–	25,000 (100.0)	4,000 (16.0)	5,000 (20.0)	13,500 (54.0)	22,500 (90.0)	16,000	Nil	13,500	2,500 (10.0)
4. Bell Metal	99,000 (100.0)	–	–	99,000 (100.0)	53,460 (54.0)	–	20,790 (21.0)	74,250 (75.0)	45,540	–	20,790	24,750 (25.0)
5. Stone Carving	34,000 (100.0)	–	–	34,000 (100.0)	30,000 (88.2)	–	4,000 (11.8)	34,000 (100.0)	4,000	–	4,000	Nil
6. Applique	65,530 (91.7)	5,970 (8.3)	–	71,500 (100.0)	53,580 (74.9)	5,970 (8.4)	11,950 (16.7)	71,500 (100.0)	11,950	Nil	11,950	Nil

(Contd.)

7. Pattrachitra	8,900 (100.0)	–	–	8,900 (100.0)	7,540 (84.7)	–	1,360 (15.3)	8,900 (100.0)	1,360	–	1,360	Nil
8. Papier Machie	18,000 (96.8)	600 (3.2)	–	18,600 (100.0)	11,000 (59.1)	600 (3.2)	7,000 (37.6)	18,600 (100.0)	7,000	Nil	7,000	Nil
9. Beads Making	20,700 (100.0)	–	–	20,700 (100.0)	10,700 (51.7)	–	8,000 (38.6)	18,700 (90.3)	10,000	–	8,000	2,000 (9.7)
10 Coir Works	7,800 (93.0)	600 (7.0)	–	8,400 (100.0)	4,500 (53.6)	600 (7.1)	2,000 (23.8)	7,100 (84.5)	3,300	Nil	2,000	1,300 (15.5)
Total	3,97,580 (95.2)	20,170 (4.8)	–	4,17,750 (100.0)	2,16,950 (51.9)	20,170 (4.8)	1,12,050 (26.8)	3,49,170 (83.6)	1,80,630	Nil	1,12,050	68,580 (16.4)

Source: As per data compiled from institutional financing agencies and the field study.
N.B. : Figures in brackets indicate percentage to the total.

towards consumption purposes. Likewise the applique artisans have utilised 74.9 per cent towards working capital and 16.7 per cent for meeting consumption requirement, though the institutions have financed about 91.7 per cent of the total loan for working capital purpose only. Similar is the case with the artisans engaged in crafts like Pattachitra and Papier machie. They have also not utilised according to the exact purpose for which the loan was being disbursed. It may be observed that the institutional financing agencies supplied the entire credit (i.e. 100 per cent) to Pattachitra unit for working capital and 96.8 per cent of the total to Papier machie for the same purpose. However, in actual practice, the utilisation was only 84.7 per cent and 59.1 per cent respectively for working capital and the balance was diverted for consumption purposes. It may categorically be noticed that none of these units were provided with consumption loan by institutional financing agencies.

As against this, all other sample artisan units studied showed a utilisation gap, arising out of the amount of the difference between loan supplied by institutional financing agencies and amount of loan utilised by sample artisan units. Table 5.9 shows that the artisans engaged in the trades like pottery, bamboo works, bell metal work, coir works, beads making and weaving shows an utilisation gap. Not only that they have underutilised but also misutilised a significant portion of the loan received, for purpose other than those for which the loan was supplied.

Of the total loan supplied to the pottery units which amounts to Rs. 1.25 lakhs, the percentage share of loan utilised for working capital, term capital and consumption needs, accounted for 32.0, 6.4 and 32.7 respectively. As against this percentage share of loan not utilised for purposes other than the approved purposes stood at 28.9 Thus this 29.8 per cent was utilised mainly for unproductive uses. It depicts that the artisans have not utilised the loan exactly for the purpose of which it was sanctioned. It shows misutilisation of the institutional finance as well as an utilisation gap between the total amount received and total amount utilised. In case of bell metal artisans, the entire financing was towards working capital needs. But it was seen from the field study that they have utilised 54.0 per cent and 21.0 per cent of the total loan received towards working capital and consumption purposes, respectively. As a result there was the utilisation gap to the extent of 25 per cent, which was used possibly for non-approved purposes. It shows that the loan was not utilised for the approved purpose and also there existed an utilisation gap between the amount of loan advanced and amount of loan utilised in the artisan unit. Similar is the case with the case of bamboo works, beads making, weaving and coir works. It indicates that almost all the artisan units studies have not utilised the loan exactly according to the purpose for which it was sanctioned. It may be observed that while 21.6 per cent of the total artisans studied did not show any utilisation gap, 78.3 per cent of the artisans exhibited utilisation gap. They utilised funds for purposes other than for which it was meant.

It is further revealed from the Table 6.9 that the artisans numbering 26 who did not show any utilisation gap were mostly engaged in producing handicraft items of utility and decorative value. It is observed that there was a good demand for the handicraft goods produced in the district in general in the recent years. So greater demand for product, better marketing prospects also have contributed for a better utilisation of credit received from institutional sources. Again the location of the villages where the above mentioned artisans are living is also another contributory factor. These artisans are experiencing a locational benefit, as their villages are mostly located near the temple city of Bhubaneswar and Puri. Moreover, being situated by the side of National Highway, their products offer good marketing prospects and return. This has helped the artisans to earn a descent living. Consequently this has also facilitated for larger utilisation of funds. It may be observed as the artisan units vary according to items produced, raw material used and resources applied, the utilisation of loan by artisans may also vary from trade to trade.

The misutilisation of loan on the part of the artisans engaged in the trades like pottery, beads making, weaving, bell metal may be attributed to a common factor like non availability of raw materials. However, it is true that the bell metal and weaving artisans are mostly supplied with raw materials from the respective Handicraft Co-operative Society and Primary Weavers Co-operative Society. However, irregular supply of raw materials, at times force the artisans to remain out of jobs. Thus being jobless for certain part of the year, they have to spend the institutional credit for some unproductive purposes or for sustaining themselves. Although the artisans engaged in the trades like pottery and beads making, procure raw materials by personal efforts from local areas, the problem is not very much different. It is observed from the field study that, in the past the village pottery workers were free to collect soil, firewood and etc. for their trade from local areas. But in the recent years, due to imposition of certain restrictions, procurement of raw materials has become a problem for them. In most of the cases, they have to purchase soil and firewood at a high price. In case of Beads making, the raw materials used are not available throughout the year. However, at the time of harvest when it is available plentily the artisans are unable to purchase the entire stock of rawmaterials and storage the same for future use. This affects the operation of their units. Unable to run the units round the year due to shortage of raw materials, the artisans for some part of the year remain out of trade. As a result, they are compelled by circumstances to utilise available finance to maintain their family and for other purposes to sustain themselves.

The problem is not just of raw material alone. In case of coir artisans, lack of proper marketing is the cause for mis-utilisation of finance by coir artisans. The artisans engaged in the trade are mostly female artisans and they do not find it easy to make arrangements for self marketing, which leads to lack of proper recycling of fund and thus again leads to misutilisation of loan and the creation of utilisation gap.

However, besides the problem of raw materials and marketing, another important factor that account for the misutilisation of fund is the seasonal character of artisan occupation. It is noticed that most of the artisan units remain out of operation for some part of the year. As for example, pottery artisans remain unemployed due to lack of raw materials caused by excessive rain, bell metal artisans face problem in getting firewood in rainy season. Similarly, stone carving, pattachitra, applique and papier machie units face bad marketing situations due to lack of tourists in rainy season. Likewise, beads making artisans fail to get sufficient raw materials during rainy season and for this the trades are seriously affected. This factor also contributes towards un-utilisation of funds properly.

Again the sample artisans, mostly belong to the poor class. When they get lumpsum amount of money in the form of loan or grant they feel tempted to spend the amount immediately for satisfying their urgent needs. They do not consider it seriously to spend the amount in the trade in which they are engaged. Consequently this has helped for non utilisation of funds by artisans.

The problem is further aggravated by the fact that not all the credit requirement of the artisan borrowers are met by institutional financing agencies. The institutional financing agencies broadly meet about 83 per cent of the credit need of artisans. For the balance, they depend upon other sources. On account of the failure of institutional financing agencies to meet the full credit need of the borrowers, the borrowers very often get tempted to divert funds for other purposes. At times, non-availability of credit in time also greatly accounts for diversion of credit by artisans for purposes other than for which the amount was sanctioned.

It is further revealed from the field study that the artisans borrowers are too innocent and ignorant to know the best use of funds. They do not know the proper use of the funds available to them. Moreover, the problems like lack of education, training, guidance and etc. make the situation worse. Besides, the supervisory activities and follow up action rendered by the institutional financing agencies is not adequate in this regard, which results in misutilisation of fund for unproductive uses.

REFERENCES

1. L.K. Naidu, *Bank Financing to Rural Artisan*, Asish Publishing House, 1985.
2. UCO Bank, Lead Bank Office, *Puri Annual Action Plan 1988-90*, Puri, 1989.
3. NABARD, *Workshop for Development of Rural Non-Farm Sector*, Bhubaneswar 1989.
4. Gopal Swaroop, *Advances to Small Industries and Small Borrowers a Practical Guide*, S. Chand & Co., Delhi, 1988.

7

Impact of Institutional Credit on the Generation of Output Income and Employment by Rural Artisans

In the previous chapter an attempt was made to analyse the working of institutional financing agencies in supplying credit to rural artisans. The study reveals that there is a considerable leeway between the demand for credit and supply of credit by institutional financing agencies. The credit gap was partly met by borrowing from non-institutional agencies. The study further highlights about the mismatch between credit received from institutional financing agencies by borrowers for different purposes for which it was sanctioned. The unutilisation of credit by borrowers was primarily due to lending agencies, non-availability of various inputs and raw materials in time and inadequate quantity, and absence of guidance and training etc. However, the percentage share of credit not utilised for the purposes, out of the total sanctioned credit was not alarming and serious. In other words, the study reveals that the borrower artisans had utilised a sizeable amount of credit for the purposes for which it was given. Accordingly the primary objective of the present chapter is to analyse the impact of institutional finance on the generation of output, income and employment by the rural artisans.

The impact of institutional finance is assessed by

making a comparison between the output, income and employment generated by the sample rural artisans in the post loan period over pre-loan period. The year 1987 has been taken as the year of sanction. In the year real financing is made available to the sample artisans units by the institutional financing agency. For sample study the artisan units who have availed financing between the month of January to December of the year 1987 have been considered. Thus the year just preceding to it i.e. 1986 has been considered as pre-loan period. And post loan period is considered by giving one year gap to the real sanction of the loan. The gap is given with a view to give atleast one year time to sample artisans to utilise their fund in their trade. Thus 1989, the year when field study is also undertaken, is considered as the post-loan period. Accordingly an attempt was made to study as to what extent the artisans had improved their economic position with regard to increase in output, income and employment during the post loan period compared to that of pre-loan period. The analysis is mainly based on a field level survey which was conducted with the help of a questionnaire for eliciting information form the different types of artisans borrowers who mostly live in cluster of villages.

It is observed from the field level survey that the generation of output by sample artisans was more in the post loan period compared to that of pre-loan period. This is observed from the Table 7.1 given below.

Generation of Output

In the pre-loan period i.e. 1986 the artisan borrowers mostly generated output out of their own resources. At times they also depended on non-institutional sources like: friends and relatives, traders and commission agents and money lenders etc. However, the individual efforts rendered by the artisans failed to generate higher output in their respective units. Consequently the larger application of institutional credit in the year encouraged the borrowers to increase output in their respective units. This can be well noticed from Table 7.1.

Table 7.1

Impact of Institutional Financing in Output Generation

(in Rupees)

Categorywise Artisans	*No. of sample Artisans studied*	*Pre-loan* period*	*Post-loan* period*	*Net addition*	*Col.5 as % of Col.3*
1. Pottery	17	66,260	93,600	27,340	41.3
2. Bamboo Works	9	66,960	42,720	(-)24,240	(-)36.2
3. Weaving	27	2,67,750	3,12,778	45,028	16.8
4. Bell Metal	25	6,13,760	8,26,720	2,12,960	34.7
5. Stone Carving	4	88,400	1,02,000	13,600	15.4
6. Applique	12	5,34,720	5,91,000	56,280	10.5
7. Pattachitra	4	19,180	28,800	9,620	50.2
8. Papier Machie	6	27,600	32,160	4,560	16.5
9. Beads Making	10	62,720	84,000	21,280	33.9
10. Coir Works	6	10,485	5,868	(-)4,617	(-)44.0
Total	120	17,57,835	21,19,646	3,61,811	20.6

* Pre-Loan Period—1986.
* Post-Loan Period—1989.
Source : Data compiled from the field study, 1989.

It is observed from the foregoing table that 120 sample rural artisans produced output which is valued at Rs. 21.19 lakhs in the post-loan period. As against this, value of output produced during the pre-loan period was Rs. 17.58 lakhs. There was thus a net increase in the amount of output to the extent of Rs. 3.62 lakhs. The institutional financing in the post-loan period has helped the artisans to bring out more output than pre-loan period where the output remained at a low level due to self financing by artisans. Between pre-loan period and post-loan period, the total output generated increased by 20.6 per cent.

Craftwise Generation of Output

The Table 7.1 further indicates that most of the sample artisan units studied have realised more production in the post-loan period. However, the impact on finance is not equally felt by various sample artisan units. The artisans who have experienced an increased output in the post-loan period belong to trades like applique works, bell metal, beads making, pattachitra, papier machie, pottery, stone carving and weaving. This is possible due to availability of finance from institutional sources. It is noticed that percentage increase in net output during post-loan period over pre-loan period was 10.5 per cent, 34.7 per cent, 33.9 per cent, 50.2 per cent, 16.5 per cent, 41.3 per cent, 15.4 per cent and 16.8 per cent respectively. It is thus observed that though all of the artisan units as stated above have improved their output in post-loan period, some artisan units like applique, weaving and papier machie have not improved their output significantly. However, it is noticed from the field study that those artisan units who have produced more in the post-loan period mostly belong to the category of handicraft units. At present the handicraft products are greatly in demand in the state as well as outside of the state. Besides these artisan units are also mainly located near urban or semi-urban areas. As a result, sale and marketing of these products have improved greatly. This has encouraged artisans to concentrate on more production.

Though it is noticed that most of the artisan units have generated more production in the post-loan period compared to pre-loan period, yet some of the artisan units engaged in the trade like bamboo works and coir works have experienced a fall in production in post-loan period. Out put of these units declined by 36.2 per cent and 44.0 per cent respectively in the post-loan period over pre-loan period.

In case of bamboo works the reason for low production

was mainly due to high price of raw materials and non-availability of these raw materials in time and in adequate quantities. Bamboo basket makers generally use bamboo as their raw materials but this rawmaterial which is mostly collected by the artisans from local forests and local areas is not available readily at present. Due to restriction imposed by the government and due to high prices of bamboos in local market artisans are forced to collect the raw materials from distance places and at a high price. Furthermore, the artisans are also seen to be financed inadequately by institutional financing agencies due to which the artisans fail to acquire more raw materials for purpose of larger production. In case of coir work the problem arises mainly due to lack of marketing facilities. The artisans engaged in this trade mostly belong to women sections and again they are found to be working in an unorganised manner. As the artisans mostly belong to the high age group, they rarely undertake marketing activities on their own accord. The formation of Coir Co-operative Societies has not improved their position in a significant way. As the societies are mostly functioning as a workshop and not in their respective houses. The sample coir women artisans found this system not very suitable to them. The functioning of societies in nearby villages has not helped much in marketing the products of coir artisans. Besides inadequate storage facility is one of the important factors for which Coir Co-operation Societies failed to provide the marketing of these products.

An analysis of Craft-wise per capita production reveals that almost all crafts with the exception of Bamboo works and Coir works have experienced increased per capita production of output in the post-loan period compared to pre-loan period. This is shown in Table 7.2.

It is observed from the aforesaid table that in the pre-loan period average per capita output of 120 sample artisans stood at Rs. 14,649 per annum. In the post-loan period per capita output of these sample artisans stood at Rs. 17,664. Between the period there was net increase of Rs. 3,015 per capita output. The percentage variation in per capita output in the post-loan period was 20.6 over the pre-loan period.

Craft-wise, almost all crafts, except the above mentioned crafts like Bamboo and Coir works have higher per capita output in the post-loan period compared to pre-loan period. Of these crafts again, higher per capita output was visible in trades like Pattachitra, Pottery, Beads making and Bell metal industries in the post-loan period. Percentage variation in per capita output over pre-loan period was 50.1, 41.3, 33.9 and 34.7 respectively.

Table 7.2
Per Capita Production

(in Rupees)

Categorywise Artisans	*No. of artisans studied*	*Pre-loan period*	*Post-loan period*	*Net addition*	*Variation % in post loan period over pre-loan period*
1. Pottery	17	3,898	5,506	1,608	41.3
2. Bamboo Works	9	7,440	4,767	(-) 2,673	(-)35.9
3. Weaving	27	9,917	11,584	1,667	16.8
4. Bell Metal	25	24,550	33,069	8,519	34.7
5. Stone Carving	4	22,100	25,500	3,400	15.4
6. Applique	12	44,560	49,250	4,690	10.5
7. Pattachitra	4	4,795	7,200	2,405	50.1
8. Papier Machie	6	4,600	5,360	760	16.5
9. Beads Making	10	6,272	8,400	2,128	33.9
10. Coir Works	6	1,748	978	(-) 770	(-) 44.1
Total	120	14,649	17,664	3,015	20.6

Source: Data compiled from the field study, 1989.

It is further noticed that artisan units like weaving, applique, stone carving and papier machie also have increased their per capita output in post-loan period by 16.8, 10.5, 15.4 and 16.5 per cent over pre-loan period respectively. The improvement in per capita output produced by these artisan units has not been very much significant.

As against these, the crafts like bamboo works and coir works have negative decline in per capita output, in the post-loan period over pre-loan period. Percentage decline over the period was 35.9 and 44.1 respectively.

GENERATION OF INCOME

Increase in output generally contributes towards the increase in income. And increase in income is required to increase the scale of operation of the artisan units. It is observed from the field study that the artisan units in general, have experienced an increase in income in the post-loan period in comparison to the pre-loan period. The table 6.3 shows the impact of institutional financing on the income generation of sample artisan units.

The Table 7.3 shows that the total income of the sample artisans in general have increased from Rs. 8.3 lakhs in the pre-loan period to Rs. 10.1 lakhs in the post-loan period. It shows that the artisan units have experienced a net incremental income of Rs. 1.7 lakhs. In terms of percentage, the percentage variation of gross incremental income in the post-loan period was 20.9 per cent over pre-loan period.

Again, with the overall growth in income earned in the post-loan period, the income earned from industrial units, for which the advance has been made, have also increased considerably. It was noticed that the total gross income earned by the sample artisan units from the industrial occupation has increased from Rs. 7.6 lakhs in pre-loan period to Rs. 8.9 lakhs in post-loan period. It shows an addition of Rs. 1.3 lakhs . In terms of percentage, the percentage change in additional income in post-loan period

Table 7.3

Impact of Institutional Financing on Income Generation by Sample Artisans

(Amount in Rupees)

	Sources of income	*Pre-loan Period*	*Post-loan Period*	*Gross addition in post loan period over pre-loan period*	*Net Income in Pre-loan Period*	*Net Income in Post-loan Period*	*Net Addition in post-loan period over pre-loan period*
1	Income earned from industrial units	7,56,110	8,86,803	1,30,693 (17.3)	6,41,000	7,56,003	1,15,003 (17.9)
2	Income earned from other sources	75,230	1,18,300	43,070 (57.3)	63,140	90,300	27,160 (43.0)
	Total	8,31,340	10,05,103	1,73,763 (20.9)	7,04,140	8,46,303	1,42,163 (20.2)

Source : Data compiled as pr field study.

N.B. : Figures in brackets indicate percentage variation in post-loan period over pre-loan period.

was 17.3 over pre-loan period, which is certainly due to institutional financing of Rs. 4.64 lakhs to these units.

Moreover, income earned from sources other than industrial units, in which the artisans have engaged themselves as subsidiary occupation has also increased. An addition of Rs. 0.43 lakhs has been made by this source. The percentage change in income between the period was 57.3. It reveals that gross addition in total income is not entirely from the industrial sources. Some portion of it, is contributed by the sources other than the industrial occupations. As stated earlier the artisan units are mostly seasonal in nature. So they make themselves engaged in various subsidiary occupations other than the artisans units.

Table 6.3 also shows the impact of institutional financing on the net income earned by the sample artisans in pre and post-loan periods. The total net income has been calculated by making a deduction of various expenses. The table shows that the net income has increased from Rs. 7.0 lakhs to about Rs. 8.5 lakhs, showing and addition of Rs. 1.4 lakhs. In percentage term the net income of the artisans has increased by 20.2 per cent between pre-loan and post-loan period.

The net income earned from the industrial units has increased from Rs. 6.4 lakhs in pre-loan period to Rs. 7.6 lakhs in the post-loan period. This shows an addition of Rs. 1.2 lakhs. In percentage term, the increase in net income between pre-loan and post-loan period was 17.9 per cent. It shows that the institutional financing to the artisans have resulted in creating more income in the artisan units.

Not only that, total income of the artisans from other sources also shows an increasing trend. The net income thus has increased from Rs. 0.63 lakhs in pre-loan period to Rs. 0.90 lakhs in post-loan period. It shows an addition of Rs. 0.27 lakhs. The percentage variation in net incremental income was 43.0 in the post loan period over pre-loan period. This indicates that some of the artisans are also engaged in activities other than artisan units. As their trades are seasonal in nature they do not get employment for full part of the year. So they get themselves engaged in other occupations.

The above discussion indicates that artisans have received larger income from both industrial as well as other sources. The income is greater in the post loan period compared to pre-loan period.

Craftwise Generation of Income

It is noticed that leaving aside 15 artisan units like that of bamboo works and coir works, all other artisan units in general have experienced greater income in the post-loan period than before. The impact on income is quite great in case of artisan units engaged in the trades like bell metal, stone carving, applique, pattachitra, papier machie and beads making. However, in certain cases the return is quite significant and in some other cases the impact on income is not very much remarkable.

Table 7.4 indicates that total gross income from both industrial units and other sources tood at 10.0 lakhs in the post-loan period as against Rs. 8.3 lakhs in pre-loan period. This additional incremental income stood at Rs. 1.7 lakhs.

Table 7.4 shows that among the crafts, total incremental income was more pronounced in artisan units like bell metal, pottery, weaving, pattachitra, papier machie and beads making. Percentage change in additional income between pre-loan and post-loan period was 24.9 per cent, 59.9 per cent, 43.8 per cent, 50.2 per cent, 60.8 per cent and 25.8 per cent respectively. As against this the units bamboo works and coir works have experienced decline in income. The percentage decline between pre-loan and post-loan period was –30.5 per cent and –31.7 per cent respectively. It is evident that most of the artisans except the artisans engaged in Bamboo works and coir works, experienced an increase in income in post-loan period over pre-loan.

Table 7.5 indicates that net income earned by sample

Table 7.4

Impact of Institutional Financing on Gross Income Earned/Generation by Sample Artisans

(in Rupees)

Sl. NO.	CATEGORY OF ARTISANS	*Total Gross Income Earned*			*Gross Income from Industrial Sources*			*Gross Income Earned form other sources*		
		Pre-loan period	*Post-loan period*	*Incremental income*	*Pre-loan period*	*Post-loan period*	*Additional incremental income*	*Pre-loan period*	*Post-loan period*	*Additional incremental income*
1.	Pottery	58480	93540	35060 (59.9)	46180	63140	16960 (36.7)	12300	30400	18100 (147.1)
2.	Bamboo Works	39800	27680	(-) 12120 (30.5)	36000	23880	(-) 12120 (33.7)	3800	3800	Nil
3.	Weaving	118690	170685	51998 (43.8)	107710	152738	45028 (41.8)	10980	17950	6970 (63.5)
4.	Bell metal	138350	172850	34500 (24.9)	120300	139900	19600 (16.3)	18050	32950	14900 (82.5)
5.	Stone Carving	45000	50400	5400 (12.0)	45000	50400	5400 (12.0)	–	–	–
6.	Applique	351900	389675	37775 (10.8)	334200	369375	35175 (10.5)	17700	20300	2600 (14.7)

(Contd.)

7. Pattrachitra	19180	28800	9620 (50.2)	19180	28800	9620 (50.1)	–	–	–
8. Papier Machie	6180	9940	3760 (60.8)	6180	9940	3760 (60.8)	–	–	–
9. Beads Making	43160	54300	11140 (25.8)	31360	42000	10640 (33.9)	11800	12300	500 (4.2)
10 Coir Works	10600	7230	(-) 3370 (31.7)	10000	6630	(-) 3370 (33.7)	600	600	Nil
Total	831340	1005103	17363 (20.9)	756110	886803	130693 (17.3)	75230	118300	43070 (57.3)

Source : Data compiled from field study, 1989.
N.B. : Figures in brackets indicate percentage to the pre-loan figure.

artisans between the pre-loan and post-loan period from both industrial units and other sources. It is seen from the Table 7.5 that the sample artisans raised a net income of Rs. 7.0 lakhs in pre-loan period. In the post loan period net income received by them increased to Rs. 8.5 lakhs over the years. Net change in net income earned was upto Rs. 1.5 lakhs. Percentagewise it constitutes 20.2 over that of pre-loan period. Among the crafts percentage change in net incremental income between pre-loan and post-loan period was higher in units like pottery, weaving, pattachitra, papier machie and beads making. The percentage change was 60.1, 45.0, 47.3, 63.3 and 24.7 respectively. As against this there was percentage decline in net incremental income in units like bamboo works and coir works.

Looking at net income earned by artisans from industrial units alone it is revealed that units like pottery, weaving, pattachitra and etc. have higher percentage of change of incremental income in post-loan period compared to pre-loan period. On the other hand units like Bell metal, Stone carving and Applique have very low percentage of incremental income. As referred to earlier, units like bamboo works and coir works have negative change in incremental income in post-loan period compared to pre-loan period. It was noticed from the field study that bamboo artisans are not getting raw materials in adequate quantities and at nearby places. Due to deforestation and restriction imposed by the government, the raw materials like bamboo have become scarce and sold at a very high price in local market. As the artisans have got no other source of getting raw materials, they have to purchase it at a higher price from the local seller, which ultimately reduce the output and income earned from the occupation in which they are engaged. Coir artisans face a severe setback in their production due to lack of proper marketing facility. Earlier they were selling this product at their door step, but in post loan period they were unable to do it. It is due to the fact that the women artisans are unorganised and moreover they do not prefer to sell the coir products personally.

Table 7.5

Impact of Institutional Financing on Net Income Earned by Sample Artisans

(in Rupees)

Sl. No.	CATEGORY OF ARTISANS	*Total Net Income Earned*			*Net Income from Industrial Sources*			*Net Income Earned form other sources*		
		Pre-loan period	*Post-loan period*	*Net addition*	*Pre-loan period*	*Post-loan period*	*Net addition*	*Pre-loan period*	*Post-loan period*	*Net addition*
1.	Pottery	49690	81540	31850 (60.1)	39090	55140	16050 (41.1)	10600	26400	15800 (14.9)
2.	Bamboo Works	34360	24680	(-) 9680 (-) (28.2)	30560	20880	(-) 9680 (-31.9)	3800	Nil	–
3.	Weaving	2970	102490	149188 (45.0)	91510	135238	43728 (47.8)	10980	13950	2970 (27.0)
4.	Bell Metal	114840	139850	25010 (21.8)	101790	118900	17110 (16.8)	13050	20950	7900 (60.5)
5.	Stone Carving	38000	42400	4400 (11.6)	38000	42400	4400 (11.6)	–	–	–
6.	Applique	297000	323675	26675 (9.0)	283300	309375	26075 (9.2)	13700	14300	600 (4.3)

(Contd.)

7. Pattrachitra	16290	24000	7710 (47.3)	16290	24000	7710 (47.3)	–	–	–
8. Papier Machie	5230	8540	3310 (63.3)	5230	8540	3310 (63.9)	–	–	–
9. Beads Making	37140	46300	9160 (24.7)	26730	36000	9270 (34.7)	10410	10300	(-) 110 (1.1)
10 Coir Works	9100	6130	(-) 2970 (-) (32.6)	8500	5530	(-) 2970 (-) (34.9)	600	600	–
Total	704140	846303	142163 (20.2)	641000	756003	115003 (17.9)	63140	90300	27160 (43.0)

Source : Data compiled from field study.
N.B. : Figures in brackets indicate percentage change over pre-loan figure.

Furthermore, it may be seen that the artisans have experienced no positive change in their income from sources other than industrial units. Whatever net income they have received, they have all come from industrial units. Net income earned from other sources is marginal only.

However, leaving aside these two types of artisan crafts the income of all other artisans have increased in the post-loan period over pre-loan period. It reveals that the objectives behind financing the artisans by institutional agencies have been realised to a large extent.

Per Capita Income

Furthermore, making a comparison about the per capita income earned in the pre-loan period with that of post-loan period, it is noticed from Table 7.6 that the artisans have earned net additional income of Rs. 958 over the period. It is due to the fact that the per capita income of artisan units stood at Rs. 5,342 in the pre-loan period and this increased to Rs. 6,300 in the post loan period. It was possible due to greater utilisation of institutional credit by the artisans.

Craftwise analysis of per capita income earned by sample artisans reveal that, units like weaving, stone carving, applique works and pattachitra, experienced a sizeable increase in the amount of per capita income between pre-loan and post-loan period. Per capita net incremental income between pre-loan and post-loan period for these crafts stood at Rs. 1,620, Rs. 1,100, Rs. 2,173 and Rs. 1,927 respectively. Compared to these units, artisan industries like pottery, bell metal, papier machie and beads making no doubt experienced a net rise in per capita income between pre-loan and post-loan period, but this was relatively at a lower level. The two trades like bamboo basket making and coir works however experienced a negative decline in net per capita income to the extent of Rs. –1,076 and Rs. –496 between pre-loan and post-loan period.

As stated earlier these particular type of artisan units

Table 7.6
Impact of Institutional Financing on the Per Capita Income

(in Rupees)

Categories of Artisans Unit	*No. of artisans studied*	*Total net income in pre-loan period*	*Per capita income in pre-loan period*	*Total net income in post-loan period*	*Per capita income in post-loan period*	*Net addition to per capita income in post-loan period*	*% in post-loan period over pre-loan period*
1. Pottery	17	39090	2299	55140	3244	945	41.1
2. Bamboo Works	9	30560	3396	20880	2320	(-) 1076	(-) 31.6
3. Weaving	27	91510	3389	135238	5009	1620	47.7
4. Bell Metal	25	101790	4072	118900	4756	684	16.8
5. Stone Carving	4	38000	9500	42400	10600	1100	11.6
6. Applique	12	283300	23608	309375	25781	2173	9.2
7. Pattrachitra	4	16290	4073	24000	6000	1927	47.3
8. Papier Machie	6	5230	872	8540	1423	551	63.4
9. Beads Making	10	26730	2673	36000	3600	297	34.6
10 Coir Works	6	8500	1417	5530	921	(-) 496	(-) 34.9
Total	120	641000	5342	756003	6300	958	17.9

Source: Data compiled from field study, 1989.

have experienced less income due to shortfall of total output generated. It further indicates that handicraft artisan industries have experienced increased per capita income in the post-loan period. Beads making and pottery units have also experienced an increase in income, which is mostly due to good demand and better production. Again they are mostly seen to be working in an organised manner. Being organised they get facilities of better institutional financing, better supply of raw materials, marketing facilities, and production orders etc.

Moreover, the artisan units which are located very near to urban areas and semi-urban areas have also experienced more per capita income in relation to those units which exist in rural areas and are located far away from town areas.

So, it indicates that 105 artisans, out of 120 sample artisans units studied, have realised a positive change in their earnings in the post-loan period. In terms of percentage about 87.5 per cent of the artisans units studied are seen to have realised an increase in their per capita income. As against this, only 12.5 per cent of artisans have experienced a short-fall in their per capita income.

Return of Investment

The amount invested need to have a return of its own. The artisans investing money in their crafts need to be assured of a fair and reasonable return. The table 7.7 shows that return on investment by sample artisans. It shows the improvement in income by sample artisans utilising the bank credit in their trade, per month and per financing of Rs. 100. Thus it reveals that financing upto Rs. 100 per month has contributed towards Rs. 2.29 on an average per month in post loan period. This is seen from Table 7.7.

However, the return is highest in case of weaving followed by Pattachitra, Beads making and Applique. In all other cases the return varies between Rs. 1.08 to Rs. 1.48. In case of Bamboo works and Coir works the return is very much negative.

Table 7.7

Return on Investment of the Sample Artisans

(in Rupees)

	Types of Artisans	*Total financial assistance*	*Total net incremental income*	*Net incremental income per month*	*Return on investment per Rs. 100 per month*
1.	Pottery	124750	16050	1338	1.07
2.	Bamboo Works	6900	(-)9680	(-)807	(-)11.69
3.	Weaving	25000	43728	3644	14.57
4.	Bell Metal	99000	17110	1426	1.44
5.	Stone Carving	34000	4400	367	1.08
6.	Applique	71500	26075	2173	3.04
7.	Pattachitra	8900	7710	643	7.21
8.	Papier Machie	18600	3310	276	1.48
9.	Beads Making	20700	9270	773	3.73
10.	Coir Works	8400	(-)2970	(-)248	(-)2.95
	Total	417750	115003	9584	2.29

Source: Data compiled as per sample study.
N.B.: For Col. 2 See table 6.6 Chapter VI
For Col. 3 See table 7.5 Chapter VII
For Col. 4 is calculated dividing total net incremental income with number of months in a year.

Impact on Artisans Lifted Above Poverty Line

The impact of institutional financing on the standard of living of the artisan units studied, may very well be calculated by taking the poverty line concept into consideration. The Table 7.8 shows the number of artisan units lifted above poverty line in the post-loan period. It shows that 23 artisan units were having an annual income of about Rs. 6,400 in pre-loan period, whereas the number had increased to 33 in the post-loan period showing an addition of 10 new artisan families over the period. Number

Table 7.8
Number of Families Lifted Above the Poverty Line

(in Rupees)

CATEGORIES OF ARTISANS UNIT	*Pre-loan Period*							*Post-loan Period*						
	Below Rs. 1000	*1001-2000*	*2001-3500*	*3501-5000*	*5001-6400*	*6401 & above*	*Total*	*Below Rs. 1000*	*1001-2000*	*2001-3500*	*3501-5000*	*5001-6400*	*6401 & above*	*Total*
1. Pottery	2	7	5	2	–	1	17	2	5	–	7	2	1	17
2. Bamboo Works	–	1	1	7	–	–	9	–	2	4	3	–	–	9
3. Weaving	–	4	8	11	3	1	27	–	1	3	8	10	5	27
4. Bell Metal	1	–	9	5	4	6	25	–	1	6	5	4	9	25
5. Stone Carving	–	–	–	–	1	3	4	–	–	–	–	1	3	4
6. Applique	–	–	–	2	–	10	12	–	–	–	1	–	11	12
7. Pattrachitra	–	–	–	2	–	2	4	–	–	–	1	–	3	4
8. Papier Machie	–	6	–	–	–	–	6	–	5	–	1	–	–	6
9. Beads Making	–	2	5	2	1	–	10	–	1	2	5	1	1	10
10 Coir Works	1	1	4	–	–	–	6	3	1	2	–		–	6
Total	4	21	32	31	9	23	120	5	16	17	31	18	33	120

Source : Data compiled from field study, 1989.

N.B. : Poverty line was Rs. 6,400 per person per year during the Seventh Plan. In the Eighth Five-Year Plan, this has been increased to Rs. 7,200 per person, per year.

of artisans having income per annum between Rs. 5,001 and Rs. 6,400, increased from 9 in the pre-loan period to 18 in the post-loan period, showing an increase of 9 new artisan families in this income range. So the income range between Rs. 5,001 and Rs. 6,400 and above is showing an increase of 19 artisans over the period. The Table 7.8 shows further that this switchover to greater income category is quite significant in case of artisan units engaged in the trade like bell metal, weaving and applique units.

Impact on Employment

Impact of institutional financing is not only felt in the field of output and income generation but also in the field of employment generation. The artisan units are of such type that they mostly employ their own family members in their trade. Moreover, if required they also occasionally employ hired labour either on full-time or part-time basis in their trade.

Table 7.9 shows that the impact of institutional financing on the generation of employment in the post-loan period. The table shows that the sample artisan units have employed 465 labourers both consisting of family labourers and hired labourers in pre-loan period. This increased to 491 labourers in post-loan period, showing an additional increase in employment of 26 persons. In percentage term the increase in the number of additional labour employed constitute 5.6 per cent over the period. It reveals that the financing has resulted in improving the number of labour employed in the artisan units in general.

Table 7.9 further shows the number of family labourers and hired labourers employed by sample artisans in the pre-loan period and post-loan period. As observed from the table, the artisans mostly employed family labourers in their occupation. They depend on hired labourers to a lesser degree. The table shows that of the total 465 labourers employed, the sample artisan units employed 353 family labourers and 112 hired labourers in pre-loan period. Again

Table 7.9
Impact of Institutional Financing on Employment Generation

Employment	*No. of labourers employed*			*Man-days employed per month (8 hrs. = 1 Man-days)*		
	Pre-loan period	*Post-loan period*	*Net addition**	*Pre-loan Period*	*Post-loan Period*	*Net addition**
1. Family labour						
(a) Full time	287	281	(-) 6	6089	5877	-212
	(61.7)	(57.2)	(-) (3.9)	(68.6)	(63.8)	(-) 3.5
(b) Part time	66	81	15	836	1097	259
	(14.2)	(16.5)	(22.7)	(9.4)	(11.8)	(30.9)
Total a + b	353	362	9	6927	6974	47
	(75.9)	(73.7)	(2.5)	(78.1)	(75.6)	(0.5)
2. Hired labour						
(a) Full time	80	88	8	1438	1596	158
	(17.2)	(17.9)	(10.0)	(16.2)	(17.3)	(11.0)
(b) Part time	32	41	9	510	653	143
	(6.9)	(8.4)	(28.1)	(5.8)	(7.1)	(28.0)
Total a + b	112	129	17	1948	2249	301
	(24.1)	(26.3)	(15.1)	(21.9)	(24.4)	(15.5)
Grand Total	465	491	26	8875	9223	348
	(100.0)	(100.0)	(5.6)	(100.0)	(100.0)	(3.9)

Source : Data compiled from field study.

N.B. : (i) Figures in brackets indicate percentage to the total.

(ii) *Col. 4 and 7 figures in brackets indicate percentage change in post-loan period over pre-loan period.

in the post loan period, of the total 491, 362 are family labourers and 129 are hired labourers. It indicates that about 75.9 and 73.7 per cent of the total labour employed in the pre loan and post loan period respectively belong to the category of family labourers. As against this the proportion of hired labourers employed stood at 24.1 per cent and 26.3 per cent respectively in the pre-loan period and post loan period. It is further noticed that of the total 26 additional person employed between pre-loan and post-loan period the share of family labourers was 9 and that of hired labourers was 17.

Looking at man-days of employment generated by artisan units, it is noticed that in the pre-loan period total man-days of employment stood at 8,875 man-days. This increased to 9,223 man-days in the post-loan period, showing an addition of 348 man-days. Percentwise variation in man-days was 3.9 over the period. Of the man-days employment in the pre-loan period, family labourers accounted for 6,927 man-days and hired labourers accounted for 1,948 man-days. Percentagewise, family labours accounted for 78.1 while hired labours accounted for 21.9 of total man-days in the pre-loan period. In the post loan period, the proportion out of the total stood at 75.6 per cent and 24.4 per cent respectively. The net addition to man-days created between pre-loan and post-loan period reveals that whereas family labours accounted for 47 additional man-days, the same was 301 additional man-days for hired labourers. This shows that net additional man-days created by family labours was only 0.5 per cent, whereas the same was 15.5 per cent for hired labours between pre-loan and post-loan period.

It is noticed that both the percentage increase in number of family labourers and man-days employed by the artisans was less compared to that of hired labourers. It is observed that the post-loan period the number of part-time labour and mandays employment generated by them have increased significantly. Reason may be attributed to the fact that the number of family labourers who are actively participating in the industrial activities earlier had been declining. It may also be due to reasons like lack of interest from the younger generation in the family; lack of active participation from the older group; and preference for accepting employment with less physical labour etc.

It may be observed that the younger group of the artisan households are less interested in the trade. As the sample artisans themselves are mostly illiterate, they want their children to be educated and want to send them to school and colleges. Most of the artisan loanees have inherited the trade from their fore-fathers or from the elderly family members, but the younger group, at present, are not in a mood to follow their parents in toto. It is noticed that they do not consider it worthwhile to learn the craft from their parents. They were interested to change to other occupations, which will give sure and certain income and which will be less vulnerable to change in demand. They all have respect for their traditional occupation, but do not like to remain in the family trade for whole life, like their fathers and fore-fathers. The older generation have greater sincerity and commitment towards the profession but their number is fast declining due to old age and physical ailments.

Due to these reasons the sample artisans studied have shown a greater interest for employing hired labours on full time basis and part time basis. The Table 7.9 shows the same fact. It shows that the decrease in number of family labour on full time basis is compensated by the increase in number of hired labour employed on full time basis. The number of full time family labour which was 287 in the pre-loan period was reduced to 281 in the post-loan period whereas the addition to full time hired labour has increased from 80 to 88 from pre-loan to post-loan period. Thus, this difference is more or less compensated by the growth in employment of hired labour on full time basis. This is also true with the man-days employed. The total man-days employed by full time family labourers had declined from 6,089 in pre-loan period to 5,877 in post-loan period. The decrease of 212 man-days, is seen along with increase of 158 man-days employment by full time hired labour. So there has been a significant increase in the employment of hired labourers in the artisan units studied in general.

However, the increase in number of labourers and man-days employed including both part time and full time shows that the net addition in post loan period is not quite significant. It is noticed that in post loan period both number of labourers and man-days employed have increased by 5.6 and 3.9 per cent respectively over the pre-loan period. So, the impact on generation of employment experienced by the sample artisans is not significant.

Craftwise Generation of Employment and Man-days of Employment Created

While making a discussion about the pattern of labour employed and man-days of employment created by the sample artisans it is noticed that the impact is not uniformly felt by the various sample artisans. Impact of bank financing on employment generation in relation to various craft is shown in the Table 7.10.

The table shows that to the total number of labours employed in the pre-loan period, full time family labourers accounted for 61.7 per cent, and the part time family labourers accounted for 14.2 per cent. Compared to this full time and part time hired labourers in the pre-loan period stood at 17.2 per cent and 6.9 per cent respectively. In the post-loan period, full time and part time family labour stood at 57.2 per cent and 16.5 per cent respectively. On the otherhand, full time and part time hired labourers stood at 17.9 per cent and 8.3 per cent respectively. This indicates that in post-loan period, the proportion of full time and part time hired labourers has increased over the pre-loan.

Craftwise employment generated in pre-loan period indicates that in artisan units like, pottery, weaving, bell metal and applique, the total number of family and hired

Table 7.10

Impact on Institutional Finance on Number of Labour Employed

Artisan Units	Pre-loan Period						Total family labour+ hired labour	Post-loan Period						Total of family labour & hired labour	Net addition		
	Family Labour			Hired Labour				Family Labour			Hired Labour						
	FT *	PT *	Total	FT	PT	Total		FT	PT	Total	FT	PT	Total		Family labour	Hired labour	Total labour
1. Pottery	33	14	47 (13.3)	–	–	–	47 (10.1)	32	20	52 (14.4)	–	–	–	52 (10.6)	5	–	5
2. Bamboo Works	22	6	28 (7.9)	–	–	–	28 (6.0)	22	6	28 (7.7)	–	–	–	28 (5.7)	–	–	–
3. Weaving	65	20	85 (24.0)	–	–	–	85 (18.3)	69	35	104 (28.7)	–	–	–	104 (21.2)	19	–	19
4. Bell Metal	67	–	67 (18.9)	70	–	70 (62.5)	137 (29.5)	58	–	58 (16.0)	74	–	74	132 (26.9)	(-) 9	4	(-) 5
5. Stone Carving	5	–	5 (1.4)	2	7	9 (8.0)	14 (3.0)	5	–	5 (1.4)	3	10	13	18 (3.7)	–	4	4
6. Applique	32	15	47 (13.3)	3	25	28 (25.0)	75 (16.1)	32	15	47 (13.0)	3	31	34	81 (16.5)	–	6	6
7. Pattrachitra	6	1	7 (1.9)	5	–	5 (4.5)	12 (2.6)	6	–	6 (1.7)	5	–	5	11 (2.2)	(-) 1	–	(-) 1

(Contd.)

8. Papier Machie	9	3	12 (3.3)	–	–	–	12 (2.6)	9	2	11 (3.0)	–	–	–	11 (2.2)	(-) 1	–	(-) 1
9. Beads Making	42	–	42 (11.8)	–	–	–	42 (9.0)	42	–	42 (11.6)	–	–	–	42 (8.6)	–	–	–
10 Coir Works	6	7	13 (3.6)	–	–	–	13 (2.8)	6	3	9 (2.5)	3	–	3	12 (2.4)	(-) 4	3	1
Total	287 (61.7)	66 (14.2)	353 (75.9)	80 (17.2)	32 (6.9)	112 (24.1)	465 (100.0)	281 (57.2)	81 (16.5)	362 (73.7)	88 (17.9)	41 (8.3)	129 (26.2)	491 (100.0)	9 (34.6)	17 (65.4)	26 (100.0)

Source : Data compiled from field study.
Figures in brackets indicate percentage to the total
* F.T. = Full Time, * P.T. = Part Time

labourers employment is maximum. It is noticed from Table 6.10 that the percentage distribution of aggregate labourers to the total in the pre-loan period stood at 10.1 per cent, 18.3 per cent, 29.5 per cent and 16.1 per cent respectively. As against this, the percentage distribution of family and hired labourers in other crafts is less than 10 per cent to the total in the pre-loan period. In the post-loan period, percentage distribution of both family and hired labourers to the total was 10.6 per cent, 21.2 per cent. 26.9 per cent and 16.5 per cent respectively in the aforesaid artisan units. The percentage distribution of family and hired labourers to the total in case of other crafts continued to remain at the low level. This clearly indicates that after getting institutional credit, artisan units like pottery, weaving, bell metal and applique could succeed in employing higher percentage of family and hired labourers. Other crafts no doubt managed to employ higher percentage of family and hired labourers in the post-loan period over pre-loan period, yet it is not very significant compared to aforesaid units.

Table 7.10 further indicates about net additional employment generated between pre-loan and post-loan period. While family labourers accounted for 34.6 per cent, hired labourers accounted for 65.4 per cent of total net incremental employment created between pre-loan and post-loan period.

Impact on Mandyas Employed Craftwise

Mandays employed by the various types of artisan units before and after the receipt of the loan is revealed from the Table 7.11. However, impact on man-days employed by the sample artisans per month depicts almost the same trend, like that exists in case number of persons employed.

Table 7.11 reveals that total mandays employed have increased from 8,875 to 9,223 showing a net addition of 348 mandays. In percentage term the net addition in post loan period to that of pre-loan period stood at 3.9 per cent. The table further indicates that of the total mandays employed

Table 7.11

Impact on Institutional Financing on Man-days Employed Per Month

(8 hours = 1 Man-day)

Artisan Units	*Man-days employed per month in pre-loan period*						*Total family labour+ hired labour*	*Man-days employed per month in post loan period*						*Total of family labour & hired labour*	*Net addition to Man-days*		
	Family Labour			*Hired Labour*				*Family Labour*			*Hired Labour*						
	*FT **	*PT **	*Total*	*FT*	*PT*	*Total*		*FT*	*PT*	*Total*	*FT*	*PT*	*Total*		*Family labour*	*Hired labour*	*Total labour*
1. Pottery	790	150	940	–	–	–	940	720	228	948	–	–	–	948	8	–	8(0.9)
2. Bamboo Works	440	70	510	–	–	–	510	420	70	490	–	–	–	490	(-) 20	–	(-) 20 (-40.8)
3. Weaving	1500	190	1690	–	–	–	1690	1585	310	1895	–	–	–	1895	205	–	205 (12.1)
4. Bell Metal	1064	–	1064	1048	–	1048	2112	934	–	934	1266	–	1266	2200	-130	+218	88 (4.2)
5. Stone Carving	150	–	150	90	105	195	345	150	–	150	90	169	259	409	–	64	64 (18.5)
6. Applique	960	300	1260	90	375	465	1725	960	300	1260	90	469	559	1819	–	94	94 (5.5)

(Contd.)

7.	Pattrachitra	160	–	160	90	–	90	250	145	75	220	90	–	90	310	60	–	60 24.0)
8.	Papier Machie	270	15	285	–	–	–	285	270	30	300	–	15	15	315	15	15	30 (10.5)
9.	Beads Making	575	–	575	–	–	–	575	575	–	575	–	–	–	575	–	–	-(-)
10.	Coir Works	180	113	293	12	30	150	443	118	84	202	60	–	60	262	(-) 91	(-) 90	-181 (-5.9)
	Total	6089 68.6)	838 (9.4)	6927 (78.1)	1438 (16.2)	510 (5.8)	1948 (21.9)	8875 (100.0)	5877 (63.7)	1097 (11.9)	6974 (75.6)	1596 (17.3)	653 (7.1)	2249 (24.4)	9223 (100.0)	47 (13.5)	301 (86.5)	348 (100.0)

Source : Data compiled from field study, 1989. Figures in brackets indicate per cent to the total.
F.T. = Full Time, P.T. = Part Time
* Figures in brackets indicate percentage variation in post loan over pre-loan period.

in pre-loan period, full time family labourers accounted for 68.6 per cent. As against this the part time family labourers accounted for 9.4 per cent. Compared to this the man-days employed by full time and part time hired labourers stood at 16.2 and 5.8 per cent respectively. The situation has however undergone a change in the post loan period. In the post loan period mandays employed by full time and part time family labourers account for 63.7 and 11.9 per cent respectively. As against this full time and part time hired labour accounted for 17.3 and 7.1 per cent of the total man-days generated. This indicates that over the period the proportion of man-days created by full time and part time hired labour has gone up over the period.

Craftwise man-days generated in pre-loan and post-loan period indicates that the artisans engaged in the trade like bell metal, weaving, applique, stone carving, pattachitra and papier machie have generated more man-days in the post loan period. They were employing 2,112, 1,690, 1,725, 345, 250 and 285 man-days in the pre-loan period respectively. The man-days employed increased to 2,200, 1,895, 1,819, 409, 310 and 315 man-days in the post-loan period respectively. The percentage change in post-loan period over that of pre-loan period constitute upto 4.2, 12.1, 5.5, 18.5, 24.0, and 10.5 per cent respectively. In case of above mentioned artisan units, the additional mandays are mostly generated by employment of hired labour in post-loan period. Except the units like weaving and pattachitra the rest units like bell metal, stone carving and applique have generated more mandays due to employment of hired labourers. The net addition over the pre-loan period stood at 218, 64, and 94 respectively. Again in case of bell metal craft in particular, the addition of 218 hired labour man-days is exclusively made by hired labourers which has largely compensated the loss of family labourers upto 130 in post-loan period. As stated earlier the reason is attributed to the facts like, decreased participation or inadequate interest shown by younger groups.

As against this units like pottery have experienced very marginal improvement which is only up to 0.9 per cent in post loan period over pre-loan period. Whereas in case of artisans engaged in the trade like Beads making, no addition has been made in total man-days in post-loan period. However, the impact is quite negative in case of artisan units engaged in the trade like Coir works and Bamboo works. The percentage reduction in the post loan period to that of pre-loan period thus stood at 40.8 per cent and 5.9 per cent respectively. It is mostly attributed to the fact that due to lower generation of output and income their man-days generation has been very much reduced. It is a point to note here that although the number of labour remained constant, the mandays employed in post loan period has gone down in case Bamboo artisans. It is due to the fact that they have not effectively used the existing labour force which may be due to lack of raw materials and marketing etc.

Besides these two types of artisan craft units all the sample artisans units have generated more employment in post-loan period which is mostly due to increase in income and output in post-loan period, which may be again due to the presence of factors like good marketing, easy supply of raw materials and easy financing made available etc.

It may however be concluded that though the artisan units in general have generated more labour and more mandays in post-loan period over that of pre-loan period. As sated earlier (Table 7.9) in the post-loan period the number of labourers employed and number of man-days generated have increased by 5.6 per cent and 3.9 per cent respectively. It shows that percentage increase in man-days is less than that of increased in number of labour employed. It is mostly due to the fact that the impact of institutional financing has resulted in improving the number of labourers but the labourers employed appears to be not effectively employed, which may be due to bad marketing, shortage of raw materials, and lack of storage etc.

Per Artisan Household Labour and Man-days Employed

While making a discussion about labour employed and man-days employed per sample artisan household, it is noticed from Table 7.12 that the number of labour employed per household which was 3.9 persons in the pre-loan period has increased to 4.1 persons in the post loan period. Again the man-days employed per sample artisan household which was 74.0 man-days in pre-loan period has increased to 76.9 man-days showing a net addition of 2.9 man-days. It reveals that labourers employed per artisan unit and the mandays employed has shown an increasing trend. It indicates that artisan units have not employed more persons and have also involved themselves in this work to a greater magnitude than before as their intensity of work has increased in course of time.

Craftwise discussion about the labourers employed and man days employed showed that the artisan units mostly employed 4 persons, in general both in pre-loan and post-loan periods. But in certain crafts like applique, stone carving, weaving, the labourers employed per artisan household has increased from 6.2, 3.5, 3.1 persons in pre-loan period to 6.6, 4.5 and 3.7 persons respectively in post-loan period, while in all other artisan units the impact is mostly absent or negligible.

While estimating man-days employed per artisan household per month it is noticed that artisan households in general are employing 74 man-days per month in pre-loan period. However, it varies between 40.8 and 143.8 man-days per month and per artisan household in that period. In the post-loan period, man-days employed per sample artisan household stood at 76.9 per month. However, it is noticed that artisan units like that of bell metal, stone carving, applique, and parttachitra are seen to be generating more mandays per their units in post loan period, whereas the impact is mostly negligible in case other artisan units.

Table 7.12

Impact on Institutional Financing as Per Artisan Household Labour and Man-days Employed

Type of Sample Artisans	*Pre-loan Period (8 hrs. = 1 man-days)*					*Post-loan Period (8 hrs=1 mandays)*				*Net addition over pre-loan period*			
	No. of units studied	*No. of labour emplo-yed*	*No. of man-days emplo-yed*	*Labour emplo-yed per house-hold**	*Mandays employ-ment created per house-hold**	*Total No. of labour emplo-yed*	*Total No. of mandays emplo-yed*	*Labour emplo-yed per sample artisan house-hold*	*Mandays emplo-yed per sample house-hold*	*No. of labour emplo-yed (7-3)*	*No. of mandays emplo-yed (8-4)*	*Per artisan house-hold labour emplo-yed (9-5)*	*Per capita artisan house-hold*
1. Pottery	17	47	940	2.8	55.2	52	948	2.8	55.8	5	8	–	3.2
2. Bamboo Works	10	28	510	2.8	51.0	28	490	2.8	49.0	–	(-)20	–	3.9
3. Weaving	27	85	1690	3.1	62.5	104	1895	3.7	70.1	19	205	0.6	7.6
4. Bell Metal	25	137	2112	5.5	86.2	132	2200	5.2	88.0	(-)5	88	0.3	1.8
5. Stone Carving	4	14	345	3.5	86.2	18	409	4.5	102.3	4	64	1.0	16.1
6. Applique	12	75	1725	6.2	143.8	81	1819	6.6	151.6	6	94	0.4	7.8
7. Pattrachitra	4	12	250	3.0	73.0	11	310	2.2	77.5	(-)1	60	0.8	4.5

(Contd.)

8.	Papier Machie	7	12	285	1.4	40.8	11	315	1.5	45.0	(-)1	30	(-)1.0	5.8
9.	Beads Making	10	42	575	4.2	57.5	42	575	4.2	57.5	–	–	–	–
10	Coir Works	6	13	401	2.5	66.8	12	262	1.1	43.7	(-)1	(-)181	(-)1.4	(-)23.1
	Total	120	465	8875	3.9	74.0	491	9223	4.1	76.9	26	348	0.1	(-) 2.9

Source: Data compiled from field study, 1989.

$$\text{* Labour employed per household} = \frac{\text{Labour employed}}{\text{No. of sample units}}$$

$$\text{* Mandays employed per household} = \frac{\text{Mandays employed}}{\text{No. of sample units}}$$

Furthermore the impact is quite negative in case of bamboo workers and coir workers.

It shows that per artisan household, the man-days employed per month, in post-loan period to that of pre-loan period has improved. However, it is noticed that the improvement in labour employed and man-days employed per artisan househld has not improved significantly in post-loan period.

Craftwise Comparison

From the analysis made on impact of institutional financing on employment generation in post-loan period, it is noticed that, artisans studied have employed mostly family labour both in pre-loan and post-loan period. However, in the post-loan period the additional change is quite not in favour of family labourers and full time labourers. Due to which the hired labourers mostly in the shape of part time workers are seen to have increased. In case of pottery artisans, net addition in post-loan period is mainly due to employment in part time family labour and also mandays. The bamboo works artisans have experienced a decline in man-days generated, but however, there is no change in total person employed. As stated earlier the artisans are facing a set back in their total production in the post-loan period. It seems that the labourers are not effectively employed. The present condition of employment is probably in nature of disguised employment. However, the coir artisans who have experienced a lower production, accordingly reduced the generation of employment both from the family and outside of it.

The sample weaver artisans are noticed to be the only artisans, who have employed mostly family labour. The artisans are mostly working under a society and are being supplied with raw materials from the society. Due to which they have employed 19 persons from their own family, of which 4 are employed on full time and 15 are on part time basis.

As against this bell metal artisans have experienced a reduction of nine full time family labourers and an addition of four full time hired labourers in post loan period, showing a net addition of 5 full time labourers. Reduction in family labourers attributed to the fact like early sickness and early retirement of older persons and experienced family members from the trade. The trade which need more physical and hard labour make the artisans old and sick very early. The negative growth in family labour is again due to less interest of younger groups. As revealed from the field study, younger group of the artisan family, do not feel this work to be prestigious and are interested to sift to other occupation and activities like opening of retail shops in the nearby places and etc. As a result of which the net addition to labour employment is not from family but from outside of it.

Besides, in crafts like of stone carving, applique, pattachitra and papier machie, there has been either no change or a decline in family labour and moreover there is increase in hired labour employed. The reason is attributed to the facts that stone carving is such a work where unskilled family members could not participate significantly. In case of applique, more hired labour is employed due to the fact that, there is increase in scale of operation and unavailability of any family members. In case of Pattachitra, decrease in family labour is due to again either absence of any family members or due to death or sickness of an older family labour in the family. And same is in case with women artisans engaged in the trade like papier machie. The women sample artisans engaged in the trade are mostly depending on their family members. In case of a daughter's marriage or like that, family labour employed is reduced. However, inspite of that, the artisan units stated above have experienced an increase in their income. Besides, the artisan units engaged in the trade like beads making have employed no more new persons in the post-loan period. They have employed no new artisans both from the family and even from outside of it. However as stated earlier, they have realised more production and income, which is probably due to the fact that, they have employed some of their disguised labour force properly in the post-loan period. Being financed by the local institutional financing agencies, these artisans have intensively utilised their existing labour force.

Return to Labour

The Table 7.13 shows the return on investment per labour. The return to labour in pre-loan period which was Rs. 6.02 per month in the pre-loan period has increased to Rs. 6.83 in the post-loan period, showing a net addition of only Rs. 0.81. In case of various artisan units this return to labour is varying between Rs. 1.04 and Rs. 13.69 in the pre-loan period. However, the same stood between Rs. 1.75 to 14.17 in the post loan period. The net addition in return to labour is quite significant in artisan units like bell metal artisans (Rs. 3.46), whereas in case of artisan units like bamboo works, papier machie, beads making and coir works the effect is quite negative.

Employment-Output Relationship

While discussing about the relationship between employment and output generation in relation to sample artisans, it is being revealed that the artisan units in general have employed more labour, when they are producing more. It may be said that more employment has resulted in more output and income. But some exceptions are noticed in the process of field study. The trade like bell metal craft have shown more production but employment has declined than before. It may be due to the fact that the higher production has occurred not only due to higher employment but also due to better supply of raw materials, marketing facilities, and easy transportation etc. The bell metal sample artisans are being regularly supplied with raw materials by their respective handicraft co-operative society. Again the society is also helping the artisans in procurement of finished product. So the production is becoming regular and without

Table 7.13
Impact on Return to Labour

(Amount in Rupees)

Artisan Categories	*Pre-loan Period*				*Post-loan Period*				
	Net income derived	*Net income derived per month*	*Employ-ment generation (mandays) per month*	*Return to labour (in Rs.)*	*Net income derived*	*Net income derived per month*	*Employ-ment generation (mandays in Rs.)*	*Return to labour (in Rs.)*	*Net addition (in Rs.)*
1. Pottery	39090	3258	940	3.46	55040	4587	948	4.84	1.38
2. Bamboo Works	30560	2547	510	5.00	20880	1740	490	3.55	(-)1.45
3. Weaving	91510	7624	1690	4.51	135238	11270	1895	5.99	1.44
4. Bell Metal	101790	8483	2112	1.04	118900	9908	2200	4.50	3.46
5. Stone Carving	38000	3167	345	9.18	42400	3533	409	8.64	(-)0.54
6. Applique	283300	23608	1725	13.69	309375	25781	1819	14.17	0.48
7. Pattrachitra	16290	1358	250	4.66	24000	2000	310	6.45	1.80
8. Papier Machie	5230	436	285	1.53	8540	708	315	2.25	(-)0.60
9. Beads Making	26730	2228	575	3.87	36000	3000	575	5.21	(-)0.54
10 Coir Works	8500	708	443	1.76	5530	461	262	1.75	(-)0.01
Total	641000	53417	8875	6.02	756003	63000	9223	6.83	0.81

Source : Data compiled from field study.

N.B. : For Col. 2, See Table 7.5; Col. 3, Total net income derived by 12 months in a year, For Col. 4, See Table 7.10.

any interruption. Regarding lower employment it may be stated that the present number of labour force is the desired number of labourers and the surplus labour employed in pre-loan period may be considered as superfluous employment. But in other crafts like applique works, there is improvement in employment and production in the post-loan period. This is also true with the crafts like papier machie, pattachitra, and pottery where growth in output is associated with improvement in labour employed. In case of beads making however, production has increased without any increase in employment. It is due to fact of the intensive use of existing labour force in the post-loan period.

In case of bamboo works the production is negative but the number of labourers employed remained the same as it was in pre-loan period. However, the mandays employed per month has been declining. It is due to the fact that, due to shortage of raw materials the production is not increasing but the person employed in the trade are there as before and they do not shift to other occupations and are engaged in the same trade as before and feel themselves employed. But due to negative production mandays contributed by these labourers has decreased.

Production and Profitability

In the artisan units the profit mostly depends upon the effort and skill of the artisan and his family members who are either engaged partly or fully. More the family members engaged in the trade, more will be the profit.

They even do not have anything like ploughback profit in their industrial activities as well. It is due to the fact that there is mostly no surplus and profit. The profit mostly constituted the wage component. At times the artisans divert some funds from family expenses and utilise it for production. The artisans never keep aside something like working capital needs. They allocate resources according to the day to day requirements, either in the family or in the industrial occupation. They do not spend on a planned manner. It is revealed from the field study that, they do not hesitate to cut down the business expenditure and spend it for family needs. It is due to the fact that the artisans remain out of job for some part of the year. The reasons may be adverse seasonal condition, lack of marketing, lack of raw materials, lack of adequate working capital, family emergency and etc.

Asset Formation

Artisan units mostly live from hand to mouth. They generally do not get opportunity to save for future. It is noticed that, even if they save, they do not like to save in financial institutions. But they like to save in consumer durables, construction and repairing their houses, and investing for opening a tea stall, and bittle shop etc. (T. 7.14).

The artisans are seen to have invested upto Rs. 65 thousand in the post-loan period. The proportion of physical assets and financial assets to the total amount of assets formed constitute upto 84.7 per cent and 15.3 per cent respectively. This may be seen from Table 7.14. Of the total amount spent towards the formation of physical assets, a significant portion is invested for constructing and repairing their houses. In 13 out of 17 cases, the artisans have spent Rs. 42.500 towards the above mentioned purposes. It shows that about 76.9 per cent of the total asset formed is on this field. In other two cases the artisans are noticed to have spend for purchasing items like a second hand cycle, scooter and radio etc. Bell metal sample artisans have spent some of their resources for purchasing those above mentioned consumer durables. This can be observed from Table 7.15. In other two cases the artisans have invested for opening small shops. However, it is true that the amount the artisans spend for all these purposes are not generally out of surplus. But the amount is probably diverted from the main industrial activities.

A craftwise discussion on asset formation as shown in Table 6.15 shows that in case of artisans units like pottery, it was only observed that a few among them have deposited

Table 7.14

Asset Formation by the Sample Artisans in General in Post-Loan Period

Types of Assets	*Asset Formation*				*Total (1+2)*	
	Physical		*Financial*			
	Quantities (in Nos.)	*Value (in Rs.)*	*Quantities (in Nos.)*	*Value (in Rs.)*	*Quantities (in Nos.)*	*Value (in Rs.)*
1. Physical :						
(a) Land	–	–	–	–		
(b) House (construction & repairing)	13 (76.5)	42,500 (76.9)	–	–		
(c) Durable items viz. Radio, Scooter, Cycle	2 (11.8)	8,000 (14.5)	–	–		
(d) Starting a shop	2 (11.8)	4,750 (8.6)	–	–		
Total (1) :	17 (100.0)	55,250 (100.0)	–	–		
2. Financial :						
(a) Bank deposit	–	–	–	10,000 (100.0)		
Grand Total :	17 (100.0)	55,250 (100.0) (84.7)	–	10,000 (100.0) (15.3)	17	65,250 (100.0)

Source : Data compiled from field study, 1989.
N.B. : Figures in brackets indicate percentage to the total.

Table 6.15

Asset Formation - After Receiving the Loan, Craftwise

Types of Assets	Asset Formation				Total (1+2)	
	Physical		Financial			
	Quantities (in Nos.)	Value (in Rs.)	Quantities (in Nos.)	Value (in Rs.)	Quantities (in Nos.)	Value (in Rs.)
1. Pottery	6 (41.2)	22,750 (41.2)	–	10,000	7 (41.2)	32,750 (50.2)
2. Bamboo Works	–	–	–	–	–	–
3. Weaving	3 (17.6)	4,000 (4.2)	–	–	3 (17.6)	4,000 (6.1)
4. Bell Metal	5 (29.4)	23,000 (41.6)	–	–	5 (29.4)	23,000 (35.2)
5. Stone Carving	–	–	–	–	–	–
6. Applique	1 (5.8)	5,000 (9.0)	–	–	1 (5.8)	5,000 (7.7)
7. Pattrachitra	–	–	–	–	–	–
8. Papier Machie	–	–	–	–	–	–
9. Beads Making	1 (5.8)	500 (0.9)	–	–	1 (5.8)	500 (0.8)
10 Coir Works	–	–	–	–	–	–
Total	17 (100.0)	55,250 (100.0)	–	10,000	17 (100.0)	65,250 (100.0)

Source : Data compiled from field study.

N.B. : Figures in brackets indicate percentage to the total.

upto Rs. 10,000 in the financial institutions like RRB. It is again to state that this was not out of profit, but it was from the credit supplied to them from institutional sources. It was observed from the field study that pottery artisans have been properly financed, by their industrial co-operative societies which is organised under Orissa Khadi and Village Industries Board. It was further observed that husband and wife belonging to same household has been financed individually. Furthermore, the artisans engaged in the trade feel insecure in the trade, so they prefer to deposit some of their borrowing rather than to invest in their traditional artisan occupation. As a result of which they have formed asset significantly, in comparison to that of other artisans, Besides asset formation by bell metal artisans is also quite significant. Thus the relative share of units like pottery and bell metal to the total asset formation constitute upto 50.2 and 35.2 per cent respectively in the post-loan period. It was very much negligible in case of weaving, applique and coir works. The point to note here is that the artisans who have misutilised the finance available to them are seen to have formed physical or financial assets. However, it is further noticed that bamboo works and coir artisans have misutilised their fund significantly and have not formed any asset. It seems that they have misutilised the financial assistance mostly for simple consumption needs.

The principal motive behind financial assistance made available to artisan units is to create additional income for the artisan families, as well as for the state. It was noticed that in the post-loan period the artisan families have contributed upto Rs. 1,15,003. In terms of percentage the artisans have realised 17.9 per cent of increase in income after being financed. Not only that in the post loan period the number of employment has also increased with 5.6 per cent. The growth in income and employment which is mostly influenced by output generation has also been increased by 20.6 per cent.

But it is a fact that increase in output, income and

employment could have been much greater in the reference year. It was noticed that in the recent years, due to change in attitude of customers towards hand-made artisan product, the marketing has not been a problem for the artisan units. But due to lack of proper financing to the units the artisans are experiencing a credit gap. Furthermore, the credit available to them is not properly utilised and at times the loan is seen to be misutilised for unproductive purposes. As a result of which the artisans are not able to purchase the raw materials in adequate amount, and in time. Due to shortage of raw materials and inflationary situation, the problem is becoming more greater, which is leading to seasonal unemployment, less production, and ultimately less contribution towards their own income and income of the state, as well.

8

Problems Confronted by Rural Artisans and Institutional Credit Agencies

The primary objective of this chapter is to highlight the problems encountered by rural artisans in course of their working. Besides, problems came across by institutional financing agencies in course of their lending operations with rural artisans is also ferreted out.

As revealed from the foregoing chapters, rural artisans occupy an important position in promoting the development of village and cottage industries in the state in general and the district in particular. As observed the sample selected artisans belong to both traditional and modern types of village and cottage units. In course of their operation, they have come across with certain problems. An attempt is made in this chapter to analyse these problems.

It is noticed from the analysis made in the previous chapters that there is a good deal of mismatch between the demand for and supply of finance in sample selected artisan units. On account of which most of the artisans, depended upon sources other than institutional to meet the credit needs. Again, even whatever credit was available to the artisans by the institutional financing agencies that is not fully utilised by the sample artisans. In otherwords, there is the mismatch between credit supplied to sample artisans for various purposes and utilisation of credit by them for the said purposes. The utilisation gap, though not serious and alarming yet its presence is a matter of great concern. It is further noticed that the rural artisans had utilised the funds with the good intention of generating more output, income and employment in their trade. However, it is noticed that the impact of institutional finance is well felt by only 3 to 4 artisan crafts. In case of other units the impact is marginal only, and in case of two categories the impact is negative. It is against this background that problems faced by rural artisans and institutional financing agencies are discussed.

In order to collect information from sample artisans, an opinion survey was made through a questionnaire. The information so collected broadly suggest the nature of problems confronted by sample artisans. At the same time, views of bank officials and other officials in charge of development agencies have also been collected through personal interview method. This rapport with bank officials and others has helped to elicit views regarding the type of problems they come across in course of lending. The discussions made in the following paragraphs broadly exhibit the views as expressed by rural artisans and the bank officials operating in the district.

The problems faced by rural artisans indicate that these borrowers come across with multiplicity of difficulties in course of their working.

On the Borrower's Side

***Inadequate and untimely supply of finance*:** It is thus noticed that in case of about 85.8 per cent of the artisan borrowers studied, the loan supplied to them is not sufficient to meet their entire credit needs. It is also revealed that nearly 40.1 per cent of the credit amount demanded by the rural artisans have remained unfulfilled. It is a fact that almost all the artisans studied requires not only working capital to operate their trade, but also required consumption loan for the purpose of maintaining their family in time of their actual engagement in work. But the financing institutions have only engaged in supplying working capital and term capital. So it is true that they are not meeting all the type of credit need of the artisan units.

Field study shows that finance is also not availed in time. About 75 per cent of the sample artisans expressed that the financing is not generally given at the peak season of their trade, when they require the financing most. As a result of which they have to depend upon local money lenders who supply cash loan and raw materials.

***Loan policy and credit procedures inflexible and cumbersome*:** The artisans units also face various other problems while borrowing from institutional sources. Being illiterate and ignorant enough in this matter they do not know how to fill up the application forms and to furnish the feasibility report for quick disposal of loan. The loan policy and credit procedures of banks are generally seen to be cumbersome and inflexible. The application form not only contain a number of details, but also it requires to be supported by various documents, collected from various sources, which is a difficult task. It is noticed from the field study that about 27.0 per cent of the artisans have hold the opinion that, financing from institutional sources is more time consuming and a delayed affair. Though it was noticed that almost all the artisans surveyed have shown a great preference for getting financial help from the institutional sources, yet it was noticed that 17.0 per cent of the sample artisans have still held the opinion that taking loan from the non-institutional sources is less time consuming and easy to get and is available at the time of necessity.

***Higher rate of interest on loans*:** It is seen that some artisans also face problems due to the high rate of interest charged by credit institutions. Banks generally charge rate of interest at a rate of 12.5 per cent per annum from the rural artisans. However, a limited number of the artisans are financed under DRI scheme are charged at a rate of interest of 4 per cent per annum. The field study reveals that about 65 per cent of the artisans units studied have opined that the rate of interest charged is very high and it should be made low; while only 5 per cent expressed that the rate is not very much high. However, 25 per cent of the artisans studied hold an indifferent opinion about the rates charged by institutional credit agencies. It is further noticed that the artisans who have received term capital assistance in shape of tools and equipments generally put forward a complain about the bad quality of these implements.

***Delay in the disbursement of loan*:** Furthermore, the artisans face difficulty due to certain delay in disbursement of loans. It is a matter of principle that, advancement under Rs. 25 thousands, is to be disbursed, within 3 to 4 weeks. But it is revealed from the field study that about 75 per cent of the sample artisans studied have faced problems due to this type of delay. However, about 25 per cent of total sample artisans are fully satisfied about the time and process of loan disbursement. Artisans have also expressed that the loan is sanctioned to them after repeated visit to the bank, repeated requests and approach to the bank officials. About 23 per cent of the artisans have expressed that they have got the loan amount through middlemen or local head man or pressure group and have paid commissions to them. In this situation when the bank is located at a distant place, the problem becomes more greater. Because a repeated visit to bank branch results in loss of work for some days. This is ultimately responsible for reducing income and output in the unit.

***Illiteracy and ignorance of Artisan borrowers*:** Artisans are mostly seen to be illiterate. They are illiterate in the sense that they do not even know the simple alphabets. It is noticed that about 49.1 per cent of the artisans do not even able to read and write. About only 26.6 per cent of the artisans studied have got a primary level education. The problem is quite serious in case of sample artisans belonging to women category. This has led to improper utilisation of fund, poor repayment of dues and inadequate marketing of product etc.

They mostly undertake their trade in an unplanned manner and do not reap the desired benefit.

Being illiterate and ignorant the sample rural artisans are not able to know about the various schemes and policies adopted by different organisations and institutions for purpose of financing and promoting them. It is noticed from field study that about 45.0 per cent of the total sample artisans studied have got even no knowledge about these schemes under implementation at present like IRDP, ERRP and others. Absence of publicity and extension networks in rural centres mainly contribute for this ignorance. About 35 per cent of sample artisans complained about the same. Furthermore being small borrowers in nature they feel that they do not get that much of co-operation and help from banking ins itutions.

***Absence of Training and Guidance*:** The artisans are seen to be not only uneducated, but are also untrained. It is noticed that only about 25 per cent of the total artisans studied have received training. It reveals that sufficient training facilities are not been given to the sample artisans. Due to which new innovative ideas, and creative outlook have not been properly injected into the artisan sector. Furthermore, it is also noticed that the training courses and programmes are also not rendering any benefit to the artisans who are undertaking it, because master artisans or craftsmen are mostly given training about certain traditional aspect of the craft which the artisans are well aware of it.

***Raw materials*:** The other important problems faced by the rural artisans are the problems related to raw materials, which are mostly of agro based, marine based, forest based and mineral based in nature. Due to reasons like deforestation and restrictions imposed from time to time by the government the collection of required quantities of raw materials from local areas has become a difficult job. As for example pottery artisans, do not get soil, fuel and other required materials due to soil erosion and deforestation.

Bamboo basket makers face serious problems due to non-availability of bamboos in local areas. The short supply of red and granite stones has also affected the stone carving trade. Other artisans engaged in the trade like applique, also mostly face problem due to high price rise of raw materials. In case of beads making, due to shortage of financing artisans are not able to purchase the entire quantity required at the harvesting time. About 22.4 per cent are facing shortage of raw materials due to non-availability caused by governmental restrictions and policies. And about 40.0 per cent have reported that they are not able to purchase the raw materials due to high price. Furthermore, about 21.0 per cent have got problems due to irregular supply of raw materials from the sources like co-operative societies. The weaving and bell metal artisans are working under industrial co-operative societies. At times the artisans do not get raw materials for the whole year.

To solve these problems the artisans engaged in the trade like bell metal, applique, stone carving and beads making, at times have to borrow raw materials from local money lenders, traders and commission agents. The borrowing is made in terms of raw materials and repayment is scheduled to be made in terms of finished products, produced by the artisans. It is seen that under this system, item to be produced and price to be charged and other things are pre-fixed at the time of borrowing. Even if the price is fixed by the agents or middlemen, the latter purchase the entire product at a throw away price on the ground of bad quality, and design. But whatever the case may be, the artisans are seen to be exploited to a great extent.

So it is noticed that artisans face a lot of problems due to shortage of raw materials, which is being discussed in the following table (Table 8.1). The Table 8.1 shows that the artisan units in general face difficulty in generating income, output and employment due to shortage of raw materials. It is noticed that they in general require raw materials up to Rs. 142.2 lakhs for the whole year. But actually they are receiving raw materials worth of Rs. 78.8 lakhs. It shows deficit of Rs. 63.4 lakhs. In percentage term it is upto 44.6 of the total raw materials required.

Table 8.1

Craftwise Demand for and Supply of Raw Materials

(Value in Rupees)

Category of Artisan Units	*Raw materials required per year*	*Raw materials received per year*	*Suplus or deficit*	*% to the total require-ment*
1 Pottery	70,900	35,950	34,950	49.3
2. Bamboo Works	37,860	20,160	17,700	46.8
3. Weaving	4,95,840	4,24,320	71,520	14.4
4. Bell Metal	129,24,000	67,30,500	61,93,500	47.9
5. Stone Carving	21,000	21,000	–	–
6. Applique	8,15,300	5,83,900	2,31,400	28.4
7. Pattachitra	3,024	3,024	–	–
8. Papier Machie	15,060	15,060	–	–
9. Beads Making	1,06,260	42,000	64,260	60.4
10. Coir Works	550	550	–	–
Total	142,19,794	78,76,464	63,43,330	44.6

Source : Data compiled from the field study.

N.B. : For convenience, demand and supply of raw materials are expressed in value terms.

It is further noticed that artisan units like beads making, bell metal, pottery, bamboo works and applique artisans are not getting their required amount of raw materials. The non-availability of raw materials stood at upto 60.4, 47.9, 49.3, 46.8 and 28.4 per cent in case of above mentioned units respectively. However, the artisan units like that of stone carving, pattachitra, papier machie and coir works face no difficulty in relation to raw materials. As against this all other artisan units face problem due to deficit of raw materials.

Marketing: Artisans also face difficulties in marketing their products. It is noticed that the artisans either market their products by self, through agents and middlemen, to government organisation or through Co-operative Societies. The self marketing give the artisans prospects for a good return, but it involves loss of some days of work. Moreover, they expressed the view that customers are not paying proper price for their product. This is very much true with the products produced by handicraft artisans. It is noticed that the artisans who sell their products through government marketing agencies like Orissa State Handicraft Corporation, Khadi and Village Industries Board, Orissa State Handloom Weavers Co-operative Society, and other agencies, sometimes fail to receive the expected price for their product. In the situation, when the products are sold through middlemen, commission agents and money lenders, the price received by artisans is considerably much lower. About 32 of the total sample artisans which constitute about 27 per cent of the total artisans studied, faced problem of selling their product at a unremunerative price, which affected the zeal and enthusiasm of the workers in pursuing the trade any more. It is also noticed that at times the problem of deficit in raw materials is very much linked with that of marketing. Artisans at times take raw material loan from local traders and repay the loan not in cash but through finished products produced by the artisan. Due to which the artisan do not get the remunerative price. It was noticed from the study that applique and bell metal artisans face problem of this type.

Inadequate Storage Facilities: While undertaking their trade the artisans also face certain setback due to lack of proper storage facility. Artisans carry out almost all their industrial work in their own house premises, which is mostly of very small in size. In case when raw materials are collected in large quantity and productions are made in large bulk, the house premises of the artisans do not accommodate the entire quantity and the stock. It is noticed that nearly 18 per cent of the artisans studied belonging to stone carving and pottery craft have expressed the problem of storage facilities. In case of pottery, processing of earthen utensils requires a wide space and moreover a kiln is required to make their earthen products burned. It is observed that every artisans is not having a kiln of his own. So he is forced to share a common bhati or kiln. Most of the times the artisans have to wait for other co-artisans, to use a kiln together. Besides due to lack of required space, pottery work is mostly stopped in the rainy season. The artisans like weavers also require not only a large space, to manufacture their products, but require a fire proof space to store up raw materials and finished products.

***Absence of use of Power*:** Absence of electricity in sample villages is one of the important hurdles. In the peak season when there is greater demand and the artisans are required to work day and night to meet the part of demand, most of them fail to meet the challenge due to absence of power of electricity. The artisans also need to switchover from traditional machines and tools to power driven appliances. This is particularly, more important for handloom artisans. Accordingly adequate supply of power is the need of the hour.

***Inadequate supply of skilled labour*:** In the matter of employment generation the artisans also face certain problems. It is noticed that the artisan units like bell metal, stone carving and pattachitra who want to employ more hired labourers in their trade, do not get them easily. The reason is mostly attributed to the fact that labour in these trades mean a skilled labour in the field. As the trade is mostly confined within a particular caste the artisans interested in employing hired labour face a lot of problems. Again in case they are available, they demand high wages which the artisans are not able to meet from their available resources.

***Improper definition of Artisan Class*:** Overlapping definition of artisan class often put the artisans in difficult position. It is noticed that some artisans engaged in cane and bamboo works are included both under Khadi & Village

Industries and Handicraft category. It leads to either double financing or at time no financing, at all. At times these artisans, are not clear enough about their actual status and the agencies to which they are linked. Consequently, they fail to procure desired amount of finance to pursue their trade.

Furthermore, the artisans face a lot of trouble due to functioning of so many financial and promotional agencies in the field. Being illiterate and ignorant they do not really know about the functioning of these agencies. It is noticed from the field study that the artisans are mostly unaware about their presence and their functioning.

On the Institutional Side

It is not that the artisans only face certain problems while undertaking their trade, and procuring financing from the financial institutions, but the institutions engaged in financing these units, also face certain problems. The most important problem faced by these institutions is that the artisans, do not come forward by themselves for procuring finance. As they are mostly unaware about the schemes and lending policies and procedures followed by institutional financing agencies, their participation in the process of lending operation is marginal only.

***Lack of implementation of rural development programmes*:** On the institutional front the most important problem is the inadequate administrative machinery for implementing effectively the rural development projects. Investments are mostly undertaken towards the rural artisans, without creating the other supporting arrangements. The banks feel that their duty is mostly over with the advancement of loans only. But supply of loan is also required to be linked with other facilities available in the area for the artisans units for which the financing is made. Otherwise financing made for the benefit of artisans is likely to be leaked out to better off borrowers in the locality.

This puts a greater burden on the success of the schemes or programmes meant for the artisans. But the fact is that the institutional financing agencies who supply credit do not get intersectoral linkages and coordination in decision making process and monitoring of activities. Due to which corrective measures are not being adopted and the sickness and failures among the schemes are not being checked. The problems becomes more greater due to the fact that the institutions, organisations, agencies and boards functioning in the field are quite a large in number. There is no co-ordination and co-operation among these institutions.

***Unscientific scale of finance*:** Another problem faced by the institutional financing agencies is about the scale and method of financing to the rural artisans. Which are seen to be quite faulty and inadequate. The method which take the anticipated production into consideration, is again confronted with a number of difficulties. Moreover, the operating cycle method which take into consideration, the time period beginning from purchasing of raw materials to the selling of finished goods and realising of cash, is difficult to calculate accurately. Artisan units do not go step by step. So fixation of a lead time becomes very difficult.

***Lack of proper identification of borrower*:** The steps leading to identification of an appropriate borrower are also not devoid of difficulties. Moreover, verification from Government and institutional records is also both time consuming and expensive. The field study shows that, identification of artisans is often handicapped by lack of intimate knowledge of the areas, people and their problems etc. Moreover, the decision of financing is often affected by political influences, resulting in lopsided flow of funds. Banks are mostly interested to finance, under certain popularly known activities. This type of lending led to the concentration of financial assistance among the influential borrows, of good economic background. At present, DRDA and block officials mostly undertake identification with the assistance of village level workers. Banks are rarely associated in the process of identification. As a result, viable rural artisans with good economic background are found identified as eligible borrowers to procure institutional loan meant for weaker section artisans.

***Demerit of target oriented credit*:** It is reported by the bank officials that there is a rush of applications to the banks at the fag end of the financial year., which causes improper assessment of credit. Furthermore, the application form contains a number of cumbersome details and it requires the artisan borrowers, to submit various documents collected from different authorities. However, in most of the cases the artisans without procuring all the documents submit the application forms at the time of the closure of the financial year with the hope of getting loan sanctioned quickly. puts the lending agencies in a tight corner. The desire to meet the targets set for lending a particular scheme often leads to misdirection of credit in wrong channels. Which cause wrong portfolio choice and inefficiency in banking system.

***Lack of rural orientation of bank staff*:** Field study reveals that, the financing to the rural artisans have increased both in quantities and dimension. The management of bank credit has thus called for an increased business expertise by the staff working in rural credit institutions. But it is noticed that the banking staff mostly originated from the urban areas, and got their education and training in towns and urban areas. So they do not fit into the rural circumstances where they are posted. It affects filed operation field supervision and managerial efficiency. Furthermore, supervision and follow up action becomes impossible in the case of rural artisans living in remote rural centres.

***Field Supervision and follow up action*:** The objective of institutional credit is the proper use of credit for the purpose for which it is given. There is, therefore, the need for assessing the end use of credit. For this, supervision and follow up action by bank staff is essential. This has two important merits. First, this encourage borrowers to earn a surplus for repaying the loan and will encourage recycling of funds in the banking system. Secondly, the artisan borrowers will be more sincere and attentive to use credit purposefully. This will reduce misutilisation and unnecessary diversion of credit to unproductive channels. This responsibility is mostly shouldered by the field staff who enjoys certain facilities in the form of vehicle advance, conveyance allowance and extra requisites etc. However, it is noticed that except in Commercial Banks, in Cooperative Banks and Regional Rural Banks field personals are conspicuous by absence. Even in commercial banks, except in some big rural branches, the filed staff are non-existent. As a result of this, the borrowers are not properly monitored and directed for efficient use of credit. This is responsible for improper use of credit in most cases.

***Extension and Guidance*:** Closely following the issue of follow up and supervision is the problem of extension and guidance. Which is rarely provided to sample artisans. They are essential in the sense they encourage borrowers to receive adequate information relating to various aspects of trade like sources of availability of raw material, cost of inputs, types of finance, non-credit facilities like marketing, storage and training, availability of subsidies and other benefits, and information relating to type and source of upgraded technology etc. The problem appears to be critical because institutional credit agencies do not have credit information cells in the rural branches. These cells are more frequently seen, on the other hand, in urban centres.

***Poor recovery of loan*:** Bad recovery of loan is perhaps the most important problem confronted by the credit agencies. It is required that the loan sanctioned to the borrowers, must be recovered and recycled. If it does not happen the ability of the credit institutions to create credit is seriously interrupted. It is observed from the field study that most of the artisans studied have not repaid the loan properly. It is noticed that 65.5 per cent of the loan financed to the artisans units are not being repaid. The bad recovery position faced by the financial institutions is revealed from Table 8.2.

Table 8.2

Sourcewise Distribution of Amount Overdues, 1989

Source	*Amount demanded*	*Amount repaid*	*Balance unrecovered*	*Col.4 as % to Col.2*	*Overdue outstanding*	*Col.6 as % to Col.2*
1. Co-operative Bank	103,750	45,375 (43.7)	58,375	86,3	15,210	14.7
2. Commercial Bank	113,400	27,595 (24.3)	85,805	75.7	14,520	12.8
3. Regional Rural Bank	200,600	70,954 (35.5)	129,646	64.6	22,066	11.0
Total	417,750	143,924 (34.5)	273,824	65.5	51,796	14.4

Source : Data compiled as per Institutional Financing Agencies.

The table 8.2 shows that a significant portion of loan advanced to the artisans have remained unpaid. It is noticed that the artisans have received 4.18 lakhs of loan from institutional sources of which they have repaid about Rs. 1.4 lakhs of loan. In percentage term, it stood at 34.5 per cent over the total demand outstanding. As result an amount of Rs. 2.8 lakhs is still lying outstanding with the artisan borrowers. In other words, 65.5 per cent of the total demand for loan still remaining outstanding with the borrower. However, various reasons are expressed by the artisans in course of field study. It is noticed that about 24.0 per cent of the artisans units expressed that due to shortage of sufficient surplus at their hand they are not able to repay the loan. Furthermore due to seasonal unemployment and underemployment caused on account of shortage of raw materials and marketing facilities, the artisans do not undertake the trade in a successful manner and do not earn more to pay for the loans. They opined that they do not get sufficient resources even to maintain their own family. About 70 per cent opined that due to lack of employment they have no alternative except to remain as defaulters. About 20 per cent of the artisan units who have not repaid the loan hope that the loan amount will be waived in future with the change in party in power. They are mostly influenced by the exemption policy adopted by the Central Government in recent past. Even if they are having a profit and earning a surplus, they are not in a mood to undertake the repayment. However, 10 per cent of the artisans are not intended to repay although they feel the economic necessity of repayment. They are the willful defaulters. The sample study shows that about 14.4 per cent of the total loan outstanding has remained as overdue which is mainly caused by defaulters among the borrowers.

These are the major drawbacks being faced by the financial institutions and the artisans units functioning in the district. Accordingly, urgent steps are called upon to remove the obstacles so as to improve the performance of institutional credit agencies and artisan borrowers persuing different type of crafts.

9

Summary and Conclusion

The primary objective of this chapter is to give a summary of the discussions made in the foregoing chapters. More specifically major findings arrived in previous sections are highlighted in this chapter. Besides, systematic policy measures are suggested for taking concentrated action to improve the socio-economic conditions of rural artisans so as to enable them to play a more purposeful role in the future.

The first chapter shows the importance of artisan sector in the rural areas where unemployment and underemployment is rampant. Agriculture is already over crowded and organised sector is not creating sufficient job in recent years. Artisan units are seem to be the most possible solution to tackle these problems as they create instant job opportunities with less unit cost. The Planning Commission has classified these artisan units into five broad categories like Khadi and Village Industries, Handlooms, Handicrafts, Sericulture and Coir Industry.

Chapter two depicts the socio-economic back ground of Orissa and district of Puri. It shows that the economy of state as well as the district is dominated by agriculture, which is very much not rewarding. Again state and the district both are industrially backward. However they have a long tradition of village and cottage industry sector. Though the state is inhabited by a large number of poor, illiterate, and backward SC and ST population, yet the abundant natural resources will help in development of the artisan sector. The district Puri where field study is undertaken in 120 sample artisan units reveals that artisan units are mostly undertaken on household basis, artisans are mostly illiterate, have learned the trade from their family and functions either individually or under societies. Shortage of finance is the most important problem faced by them.

As financing to artisan units is very much required, the organisation and operation of institutional financing have been discussed in chapter three. The chapter shows that financial institutions like co-operative banks is financing to artisans units through PACs and various industrial co-operative societies. Commercial Banks and RRBs are engaged in direct financing to artisans. All of them finance from their own as well as from refinancing fund availed from NABARD. OSFC and the term lending institutions finance from own as well as from refinancing fund availed from IDBI. This subject matter is discussed in chapter three.

The functioning of institutional financing agencies in Puri district is discussed in chapter four. It shows that Co-operative Banks are only engaged in financing Weaver's Co-operative Society. Their role is very limited in financing to other industrial co-operative. RRBs and Commercial Bank have only financed upto 4.33 per cent and 1.3 per cent of their total financing to this sector in 1989. OSFC finances have also declined significantly in the district. It shows that the contribution of RRB in this regard is significant.

The credit requirement of sample artisan units and supply of credit to them is being analysed in chapter five. It shows that sample artisans required working capital, term capital and consumption loan, which in total stood at Rs. 6.98 lakhs. As against this financial institutions have financed Rs. 4.18 lakhs showing a gap of Rs. 2.80 lakhs. This gap was partly met from non-institutional sources. Moreover the chapter shows the sample artisans has not utilised 16.5 per cent of the total credit supplied to them.

The chapter six analyses the impact of institutional

credit on generation of output, income and employment on the sample artisan sector. The field study shows that between pre-loan and post-loan period output has increased by 20.6 per cent, net income earned increased by 20.2 per cent, number of labour employed increased by 5.6 per cent, and man-days employment increased by 3.9 per cent in general. However 15 unit out of 120 have realised no possible change in the post loan period.

The important problems faced by rural artisans is discussed in chapter seven. Artisan units mostly face problem like shortage of finance, raw materials, storage facility, marketing, training and etc. The financing agencies on the other hand face problems like poor recovery of loans, illiteracy of artisans, delayed release of subsidy by Government, influence of middlemen and politicians and etc.

MAIN FINDINGS

The growth and promotion of rural artisan units are very much required in the recent years to tackle the problem like underdevelopment, unemployment, poverty and backwardness. They are important in the sense that they can create a process of industrialisation, urbanisation and modernisation both in rural and urban areas, which the large industries are not able to achieve so far. They can solve the problem of poverty in rural areas and so can create an atmosphere of balanced growth.

The development of artisan units are also required in the state of Orissa which is very much underdeveloped and poverty stricken. The state possesses a large potential of natural resources for developing them. The state also possesses a large network and high tradition of artisan units some of which are famous nationally and also internationally. But being poor, these artisans are seen to be trapped in the vicious circle of low productivity, low income and low employment trap. To came out of this, they require the help of institutional financing agencies.

The same trend is noticed in the district of Puri. Except sericulture all other artisan units are seen in Puri. The sample study covering 120 artisan borrowers in Puri district shows that artisan units are mostly hereditary and household enterprises in nature. Among them nearly 49.0 per cent do not know even simple alphabets. About 52.0 per cent of them are working without any organisation and 17.5 per cent are women. Almost all of them are using labour intensive indigenous technology. They encounter various problems like marketing, shortage of raw materials etc. But lack of adequate financing constitute the most important problem.

Co-operative Banks, Commercial Banks, Regional Banks and OSFC are the sources who supply finance to artisan units in the State. Co-operative Banks are seen to be supplying most of its credit to weavers co-operatives. Commercial Banks have not increased their position in the matter of financing rural artisans. OSFC financing to the artisan units are declining in the state significantly. As against this RRB financing to the sector is seen to be improving significantly. However in matter of financing both in the state and at the district level the artisan sector has remained as a neglected sector.

As against this the needs and aspirations of artisans units are growing in recent years. Sample study shows that they put forward a demand of Rs. 6.98 lakhs. The financing agencies have supplied credit up to an amount of Rs. 4.18 lakhs. It shows that Rs. 2.80 lakhs of demand for credit has not been met by institutional sources. In percentage term this constitute 40.1 per cent. The sample artisans have taken finance from non-institutional sources. But borrowing from these sources have covered only 16.4 per cent of the credit gap. The shortage of financing thus affected the operation of units. Again, whatever is sanctioned that is not utilised for the purposes for which the loan was granted. Besides there is also a considerable utilisation gap. This has encouraged the use of funds in undesirable channels.

Impact of institutional financing on output income and

employment is quite positive on sample artisans in general. The income and output has increased by 20.6 and 20.2 per cent in post loan period respectively. Number of labourers and man-days employed have also increased by 5.6 and 3.9 per cent. It shows that impact is quite encouraging but the improvement could have been much more if adequate financing and proper utilisation had been undertaken by sample artisans. Moreover, it is noticed that impact is not uniformly felt by various units. However, it is noticed that 15 out of 120 units like bamboo basket making and coir works have not fared well. In respect of output, income and employment generation, the performance of these units has declined in the post-loan period compared to pre-loan period.

The sample artisans have faced problems like dearth of adequate finance, inflexible loan policy and cumbersome credit procedure, shortage of raw materials, poor marketing, lack of training, guidance and etc. Institutions supplying credit to them also have faced certain problems like illiteracy and ignorance on the part of the borrowers, lack of credit worthiness of artisans, presence of middlemen and vested interest groups, poor recovery of loans, absence of staff to undertake field supervision and follow up action, multiplicity in schemes for the same purpose and lack of co-ordination among credit agencies leading to double and multiple financing etc.

***Policy Prescriptions*:** Looking at these issues, it is now essential to find out appropriate measures to improve the economic condition of artisan units.

In respect of the above conclusions from the field study, it is realised that, there is an imperative need to organise the artisan sector from the grass root level. It is noticed that the artisans functioning under Co-operative Societies are relatively better off then the artisans who are working individually. Ideally speaking, the process of organising the artisan units would be done in such a manner that the artisans themselves will take the initiative and will build their own organisations and shoulder the responsibilities for their development. Therefore, it is felt that one of the best method is to bring them under co-operative fold. So that they can avail the facilities of institutional credit, marketing facilities, training programme, and easy supply of raw materials etc.

Adequate facilities should be provided to make the artisans literate. They should be given both functional and formal education. Necessary training programme is very much necessary for improving their efficiency. Provision of education and training for them will create awareness among them. So they will benefit from various developmental schemes and policies. In this context, institutional financing agencies either jointly or separately conduct training programmes regularly for the benefit of artisans. Since the artisans are rural in character, the training courses need be reoriented to suit their purpose. At present, training programmes are, of course, conducted but they are more general in nature. Besides they are not conducted regularly and do not involve different categories of artisans.

Artisans generally use labour intensive traditional technology. But it is now necessary to make an improvement of the indigenous technology used by the artisans from age old time, so that their style of production, items, time required and quality of products will show marked improvement. But the change of technology need not be more advanced type, sophisticated and costly because that will be beyond the reach of the sample artisans, and will replace labour by capital. It is further required that the technology so adopted shall not only disturb the traditional art design and style liked by the general public.

In this connection, a suggestion is often made for the application of intermediate technology or appropriate technology. This need not be an imported one. This shall be developed indigenously. It will help to use capital but certainly not at the expenses of replacing labour. It will be labour absorbing but at the same time capital using. This will encourage competitiveness and efficiency of artisans units. More specifically such a type of technology has more relevance in artisan unit like bell metal, weaving, coir works and applique works etc.

Adequate and timely credit should be provided to the artisan units by the financial institutions. Supply of credit should be calculated by taking into consideration inflationary rise in prices of raw materials and other inputs into consideration. Again financing be made timely by taking into consideration the peak season of respective trades. The rate of interest charged should be lowered further and should be based on market related rate of interest. The demand for and supply of loan by rural artisans in the rural sector need ultimately decide the rate of interest more suitable for them. This will increase their competitiveness and efficiency. The present practice of giving concessional rate of interest to all need be discontinued. It must under suitable cases be enforced in favour of those whose performance in the trade is not encouraging.

Furthermore, the procedure of financing to the artisan borrowers should be made simple, clear and a shortcut one. The application forms should be printed and prepared in the regional language. As a result of which artisans will not face any trouble of making an application for borrowing loan. The process of disbursement of loan should also be made such that it will require less time at the disbursing end.

Since artisan borrowers have no knowledge about the technicalities involved in various schemes and projects, the Small Scale Service Institute (S.S.S.I.) or Directorate of Industries or Orissa Technical Consultancy Oraganisation (ORITCO) need to undertake the responsibility of preparing feasibility reports of various projects in advance so as to enable the artisan borrower to raise loans easily from institutional credit agencies by using them. The feasibility reports must contain all details like scale of finance, quantity of raw materials required, number of persons required for employment, marketing prospects, and profit expectations etc. Absence of any such information is one of the reasons for the cause of low and untimely financing by credit agencies. Once this proposal is implemented, credit will be disbursed within 3 to 4 weeks as stipulated and desired.

It is also required that the loan need be provided to the rural artisans without any pressure from any side. It is very often noticed that the credit agencies are under pressure by the middlemen and vested interest groups in rural areas who mostly sponsor artisans to banks for loans. It is suggested by a recent report submitted under the Chairmanship of M. Narasimham that both the Central and State Government need to observe certain discipline while recommending for target oriented schemes and programmes. It also suggested that credit agencies need to adopt simplistic loan policies and credit procedures for the benefit of rural artisans. They need to adopt norms of providing liberalised credit in an atmosphere of freeness and frankness. This will prevent the pressure groups to automatically remain away from adopting any pressure tactics. What is suggested here is that credit agencies need to play the role of a friend, philosopher and guide to rural artisans in all matters.

It is further necessary that the Co-operative Societies which are engaged in financing the rural artisans either through cash or raw materials should function actively without any conflict, confusion and politics. So that the assistance provided to the ultimate member artisans would continue through out the year. Proper care and attention need to be given for the proper functioning of the artisan based industrial co-operatives.

For achieving proper growth and promotion of artisan units certain suggestive measures may be discussed.

It may be suggested that necessary steps must be take to make a proper survey about the existing artisan units. Proper identification will necessarily lead to proper implementation of developmental actions, chalked out for them.

Necessary steps should also be taken to bring the

artisans into the co-operative fold, so that they will get all the benefits of being organised.

The artisans should be given some non-formal education, which will very much relate to their trade. Proper training and guidance should necessarily be rendered to them. So that they will be able to provide items having new design, style and variety. It will suit to the present market condition and will make the trade more profitable.

Exhibition and workshop-cum-sale should be arranged in large scale to render them a good marketing. The output produced by these artisan units should necessarily be marketed by State Government or by the existing promotional institutions. It will reduce the importance of the private traders and middlemen. Moreover the product produced by these artisans should be purchased by all the government departments for their departmental use. It will boost their marketing and output generation.

While exporting the artisan product the quality of the items should be strictly checked, so that it will lead to greater demand in the long run.

Prices charged for artisan products mostly in the nature of handicrafts should be kept at a reasonable level, so that a common man will have an access to it.

Shortage of raw materials which constitute an important problem, should be sorted out at the institutional level, so that it will be available in time and at right price and throughout the year.

Moreover for improving the productivity of these units some new and innovative type of technology should be developed and implemented. The technology should be such that it will not disturb the labour intensive character of artisan units.

Loan disbursement to the artisans should be made within the stipulated time period.

The repayment period should be fixed at peak season of

their trade so the burden of repayment may be lessened. The bad recovery greatly hampers recycling of fund. So the artisans who failed to repay their dues should be strictly handled. To check misutilisation the institutions should carry out necessary follow up action and supervision. Statistics published at banking circle should give a special attention to artisan sector. It should not be merged with the small scale sector.

The banks have undertaken lead bank survey, which is mostly limited to Block level and it does not give proper information about villages. Now there is a need for gathering proper information at the village level. There need be a greater integration between district level planning and credit planning and credit planning by banks and other credit agencies. This will help to bring out the true picture of rural economy and of rural artisans living there.

In order to improve the condition of the artisan units functioning in the district and the state as well they should be provided with the above mentioned facilities. From the banking point of view also there are some suggestions which have to be followed.

The credit agencies must see their presence felt in the rural areas. At present credit agencies are required to serve a cluster of villages. Villages lying at the distant places find difficult to maintain contact regularly with the credit agencies. Besides the credit agencies need to make publicity of their schemes, programmes and policies in the rural centres. In this connection the service of village volunteers as suggested by NABARD need to be implemented. In order to serve the rural areas and the clients better, the presently adopted Service Areas Approach need to be persued. Under this a branch of credit agency will cover only one or two villages for effective lending.

The staff of the bank branches should be made well aware about the facts and figures of the rural areas where they are operating. They should be adequately informed about the areas, its people and various activities persued by them. Furthermore they are to make perfect judgement about the projects and persons with whom they are called upon to involve.

Credit agencies have rendered more of working capital followed by term capital. However, the supply of consumption credit is not regular as per the need of the borrower. It is suggested that credit agencies after thorough scrutiny of the activities of artisans need to sanction consumption credit but at the same time need to see that they are utilised for the purpose for which it is given. This is also true for working capital and term capital. For this, supervision and follow up action at the branch level need be geared up. It is suggested with this context that the Branch Managers and his staff at the branch level must maintain their personal rapport with the artisans. This will ease a number of problems.

Poor repayment of credit is one of the important problems of institutional credit agencies. Almost all types of borrowers including rural artisans in the rural areas have this difficulty. Poor repayment on the part of rural artisans is not solely due to their negligence, but mostly due to their poor economic condition. Hence it is necessary on the part of institutional credit agencies to reorient their repayment schedules. Artisan borrowers need be educated and trained to repay loans regularly, as this will give them an opportunity to borrow frequently from the lending agencies. For this, monitoring of end use of credit by credit agencies is essential.

Besides, for the generation of surplus income by the artisan borrowers both credit agencies and developmental agencies need to provide complementary inputs to artisan borrowers. For willful defaulters, wherever necessary legal action be instituted to recover loans. While sanctioning loan, the credit agencies must see that loans do create assets for the borrowers. Once assets are possessed that will encourage them to engage in viable occupational activities.

It is often observed that at the time of fixing the terms of repayment the banks should take the peak time of trade into consideration. This is required to be implemented mostly in case of fixing the repayment of the working capital loan. So repayment schedule should not be fixed on monthly or quarterly basis as far as possible.

To achieve all these goals the banks should be properly staffed. More particularly at the present juncture there is need for having field staff in the rural branches of credit agencies. They should have a cell of specially recruited-trained young men and women for this matter. The banks may have a cadre of locally recruited field assistants for supervising for rural lending programmes.

Supply of information and guidance is one of the areas which requires utmost attention. In fact there are a number of schemes and programmes having a direct bearing on rural artisans. The rural artisans fail to reap the advantages of these programmes due to their ignorance. On the side of institutional credit agencies, supply of information and guidance about the schemes and programmes is lacking. It is, therefore, suggested that the credit agencies need to have credit information and guidance cells in branches operating at the block level. Besides, these cells must also discharge the responsibility of counseling on matters vital to artisans interest.

In line with district level consultative committee, block level consultative committee be established. This will help for the integration of block level planning with credit planning at the block level, a matter which is now traced more in the recent plan documents. In the block level consultative committee, matters relating to small borrowers including rural artisans need be fully discussed. At the same time efforts need also be made to meet both financial and non-financial requirements of the artisan borrowers. For this the block level consultative committee must ensure full co-operation of the developmental agencies and credit agencies at the block level. Wherever possible, rural artisans with good reputation need be associated in the discussions held in the block level consultative committees.

It is often found difficult to obtain data and information on artisans in general and rural artisans in particular. The data published by the Directorate of Industries is sketchy and incomprehensive. Similarly data and information gathered by credit agencies also lack comprehensiveness. Directorate of institutional finance, Government of Orissa, do not have adequate data and information relating rural artisans. Even data and information supplied by Reserve Bank of India is not regular and timely. Besides, it also fails to go into all the aspects of artisan sector. In this connection, it is suggested that a comprehensive survey covering all aspects of the rural artisan sector need be made by Central Government, Reserve Bank of India or State Government and its agencies. This comprehensive survey need to highlight the historical background of each artisan units, its growth over time, the traits and characteristic of artisans, the schemes and benefits available for the development of rural artisans and their volume and size of expansion etc. Such a survey undertaken in the state will not only be beneficial to credit agencies in course of their operation, but also essential for researchers, planners and voluntary organisations working for the benefit of this hitherto neglected sector.

If measures as suggested in foregoing paragraphs are adopted in right earnest, the rural artisans will have prosperity. Their contribution to development of state's economy will be far-reaching.

Select Bibliography

(A) Books

Adarkar, B.N., *Commercial Banks in India after Nationalisation*, A.D. Shrof Memorial Trust, 1971.

Agrawal, B.P., *Commercial Banks in India after Nationalisation : A Study of their Policies and Progress*, Classical Publishing, New Delhi, 1981.

Agrawal, H.N., *A Portrait of Nationalised Banks*, Inter-India Publications, Delhi, 1979.

Balkrishna, G., *Financing Small Scale Industries in India*, Gokhale Institute of Politics and Economics, Pune, 1962.

Bank of India, *Financial Institutions and Economic Development*, Bombay, 1972.

Basu, S.K., *The Place and Problems of Small Scale Industries*, A. Mukharjee and Co., Calcutta, 1957.

Behari Bipin, *Rural Industrialisation in India*, B.R. Publishing Corporation, Delhi, 1980.

Bharatiya, L.K., *Towards Rural Industtrialisation*, Bharatiya Vidya Bhawan, Bombay, 1975.

Bhattacharya, S.N., *Rural Industrialisation in India*, B.R. Publishing Corporation, Delhi, 1980.

Bhat, N.S., *Aspects of Rural Banking*, Commonwealth Publishers, Delhi, 1980.

Cameron, R., *Banking and Economic Development*, Oxford University Press, 1974.

Chintnis, K.M., *Credit Appraisal in Banks*, D.R. and Co. Pune, 1986.

Dagli, V. (ed.), *Financial Institutions in India*, Vora, Bombay, 1976.

Datta, B., *Contents of Economic Growth and Other Essays*, Research India Publications, Calcutta, 1977.

Dawar, Ram, *Institutional Finance to Small Scale Industries*, Deep and Deep Publications, New Delhi, 1986.

Desai, B.M. and *et al.*, *Rural Financial Institutions*, Oxford and IBH Publishing Co., New Delhi, 1989.

Desai, S.S.M., *Rural Banking in India*, Himalaya Publishing House, Bombay, 1979.

Desai, V., *Organisation and Management of Small Scale Industries – A Systems Approach*, Himalaya Publishing House, Bombay, 1983.

Indian Institute of Bankers, *Commercial Banking*, Vol. I, II & III. Vora & Co., Bombay, 1986.

Kalakundarikar, A.B., *Regional Rural Banks and Regional Development*, Daya Publishing, New Delhi, 1989.

Khan, G., *Nationalised Banking and Economic Development*, Vora & Co., Bombay, 1978.

Lal, S., *Loans to Small Industries and Small Borrowers*, Navarang Publications, New Delhi, 1976.

Mahajan, V.S., *Studies in Indian Banking and Finance*, Vol. I and II, Deep and Deep Publications, New Delhi, 1989.

Mishra, B. and Mishra, S.N., *Rural Industrialisation*, Vidyapuri, Cuttack, 1987.

Mishra, S.N., *Growth of Commercial Banking in Orissa*, ANU Books, Meerut, 1984.

Mohanty, B., *Economics of Small Scale Industries*, Ashish Publishing House, New Delhi, 1986.

Mohanty, D.C., *Small Scale Industry in Orissa : A Case Study of Puri District*, Asish Publishing House, New Delhi, 1985.

Naidu, L.K., *Industrial Finance and Rural Development*, Asish Publishing House, New Delhi, 1985.

_________, *Bank Finance to Rural Artisans*, Asish Publishing House, New Delhi, 1988.

Commen, M.A., *Banks in the Service of Weaker Sections*, Oxford & IBH Co., New Delhi, 1980.

Panadikar, S.G. and Mithani, M.D., *Banking in India*, Orient Longman, Bombay, 1975.

Papola, T.S., *Rural Industrialisation – Approaches and Potentialities,* Himalaya Publishing House, Bombay, 1984.

_________, *Spatial Diversification of Industries – A Study in Uttar Pradesh*, Allied Publishers, Bombay, 1981.

Pattanaik, K.M. (Ed.), *Economic Profile of Orissa*, Kitab Mahal, Cuttack, 1980.

Pattnaik, S.C., *Industrial Development in a Backward Region*, Asish Publishing House, New Delhi, 1988.

Rangarajan, S., *Innovations in Banking*, Oxford and IBH Publishing House, Bombay, 1982.

Rao, R.V., *Rural Industrialisation in India, the Changing Profile*, Concept Publishing, New Delhi, 1978.

_________, *Cottage and Small Scale Industries and Planned Economy*, Sterling Publishing, New Delhi, 1967.

Savaraiah, G., *Rural Banking in India – An Empirical Study*, Daya Publishing, Delhi, 1988.

Schumacher, E.F., *Small is Beautiful – A Study of Economics as if People Mattered*, Radhakrishna, New Delhi, 1977.

Sethuram, T.V., *Institutional financing and Economic Development in India*, Vikas Publications, New Delhi, 1970.

Srinivasan, E.S., *Financial Structure and Economic Development*, Sterling Publishers Pvt. Ltd., New Delhi, 1977.

Thakur, S.Y., *Rural Industrialisation in India: Strategy and Approach*, Sterling Publishers Pvt. Ltd., 1985.

(B) Journals and Periodicals

Angadi, V.B., "Bank's advances to priority sectors: an enquiry into the causes of concentration," *Economic and Political Weekly*, Vol. 18, No. 12, March 26, 1983.

Balkrishnand, S., "Lead Banks Scheme: Problems and Prospects," *The Journal of the Indian Institute of Bankers*, Vol. 55, No. 3, July-September, 1984.

Chandrasekhar, K., "Areas in Financing Small Scale Units," *The Eastern Economists*, May 4, Vol. 68, No. 18, May 4, 1979.

Dak, T.M., "Challenges of Rural Industrialisation – A study," *Kurukshetra*, Vol. 38, No. 7, April 1990.

Das, Kumar B., "Spatial and Sectoral Configuration of Rural Industrialisation – A study," *Kurukshetra,* Vol. 39, No. 6, March 1991.

Datta, B., "Small is Big: A critic of the Industrial Policy Statement," *Economic and Political Weekly*, 1978, 13, (3).

Garg, R.B.L., "Crisis in Coir Industry," *The Eastern Economists (Supplement)*, Vol. 71, No. 23, 1981.

Ghosh, S.P., "Promoting small scale industries," *The Eastern Economists* (Supplement), Vol. 71, No. 21, November 20, 1981.

I. Satya Sundaram, "Priority sector lending problems: Prospects," *The Journal of the Indian Institute of Bankers,* Vol. 55, No. 1, Jan.-March, 1984.

_________, "Institutional Finance for small scale sector," *The*

Journal of the Indian Institute of Bankers. Vol. 55, No. 2, April-June 1984.

Krishna Iyer, S.R., "Rural Industries in the Indian Economy," *RBI Bulletin*, January 1971.

Kurian, N.J., "Employment Potential in Rural India: An Analysis," *Economic and Political Weekly,* Vol. 25, No. 52, December 29, 1990.

Mafatlal Arvinda N., "Industry pull up the rural sector," *The Eastern Economists,* Vol. 64, No. 16, April 18, 1975.

Mahajan, V.S., "Strategy for Rural Industrialisation," *Khadi Gramodyog*, Vol. XXXIV, No. 9, June 1988.

__________, "Marketing Major Obstacle in Rural Industrialisation," *Khadi Gramodyog*, Vol. 34, No. 12, September 1988.

Mallaya, M.R., "Recovery of Bank Advances," *The Journal of the Indian Institute of Bankers*, Vol. 55, No. 3, July-September, 1984.

Malhotra, R.N., "The Role of Banking in Rural Development," *RBI Bulletin,* September 1986.

Mishra, S.N., "Regional Rural Banks and Development of Weaker Sections in Orissa," *Orissa Economic Journal*, XIX, No. 1 and 1 1986.

__________, "Role of Commercial Banks in financing small artisans," *Vision,* Vol. I, 1987.

Patel, A.R., "Problems and Challenges of Rural Credit: A Case for Nationalised Banks," *Prajnan,* Vol. III, No. 3, July-September 1974.

Raina, L.N., "Coir has its place in the Economy," *The Eastern Economists*, Vol. 70, No. 24, June 12, 1981.

Reddy, G. Raghava, "Bank Finance for village and small industries," *The Eastern Economists*, Vol. 70, No. 10, March 6, 1981.

Taimni, K.K., "Relevance and Role of Handicraft

Cooperatives," *The Eastern Economists*, Vol. 70, No. 19, November 7, 1980.

(C) Government and Other Institutional Publications

(i) Government of India

Central Statistical Organisation, *Statistical Abstract*, 1986 to 1989, New Delhi.

Ministry of Finance, *Report of the Rural Banking Enquiry Committee*, New Delhi, 1950, (Chairman: Purusottam Das Thakur Das).

_________, *Report of the Banking Commission*, Controller of Publications, New Delhi, 1972, (Chairman: R.G. Sariya).

_________, *Report of the Problems of Sick Units* (Mimeo), New Delhi, 1978, (Chairman: I.G. Patel).

_______, *Report of the Committee on Financial Sector Reforms*, New Delhi, 1991, (Chairman: M. Narasimham).

_________, *Economic Survey*, 1985-86 to 1991-92, Controller of Publications, New Delhi.

Ministry of Industries, *Report of the Working Group II on Small Scale Industries* with special reference to District Industries Centre, New Delhi, 1978.

(ii) Government of Orissa

Bureau of Statistics and Economics, *Annual Survey of Industries*, 1980 to 1988, Government Press, Cuttack.

_________, *Statistical Abstract of Orissa*, 1979, 1985 and 1990, Government Press, Cuttack.

_________, *Economic Survey of Orissa*, 1980-81, 1985-86, 1988-89 and 1990-91, Government Press, Cuttack.

_________, *Structure of Small Industries in Orissa*, Government Press, Cuttack, 1969.

Department of Agriculture and Cooperation, *Agricultural Credit Projects – Banking Plan (Orissa)*, Government Press, Cuttack, 1976.

Directorate of Institutional Finance, *Banking Profile of Orissa, 1969-1989*, Bhubaneswar (Mimeo).

Directorate of Industries, *Taskforce on Handicrafts*, Government Press, Cuttack, 1977.

_________, *Statistical Handbook of Targets and Achievements in Small Scale Industries and Artisan* (1980-81, 1988-89), Cuttack, 1989.

Department of Industries & Minerals, Industrial Promotion and Investment Corporation Ltd., *New Industrial Policy*, 1980, 1985, 1986, 1989, 1990, 1991, Bhubaneswar.

Registrar of Cooperative Societies, *Statistics on Cooperative in Orissa*, 1978-79, 1980-81, 1985-86 and 1988-89, Bhubaneswar.

(iii) Reserve Bank of India

R.B.I., *All India Rural Credit Survey*, Report of the Committee of Direction, Vol. II (The General Report), Bombay, 1956, (Chairman: A.D. Gorwala).

_________, *Seminar or Financing of Small Scale Industries of India* (Vol. I), Report of the Proceedings, Bombay, 1959.

_________, *Report of a Study Group of the National Credit Council on Organisational Framework for the Implementation of Social Objectives*, Bombay, 1969, (Chairman: D.R. Gadgil).

R.B.I., *Report of the Committee on Bank Credit Schemes* with reference to Employment Potential, Bombay, 1970, (Chairman: V.D. Thakkar).

_________, *All-India Debt-Investment Survey* (1971-72), Bombay, 1974.

_________, *All-India Debt-Investment Survey* (1981-82), Assets and Liabilities of Households as on 30th June, 1981, Bombay, 1987.

R.B.I., *All-India Debt-Investment Survey* (1981-82), Statistical Tables relating to cash borrowing and repayments of household during July 1981 to June 1982 and cash dues outstanding as on 30th June 1982, Bombay, 1987.

_________, *Loan Policy and Procedural Arrangements in relation to the Institutional Credit System in India*, Bombay, 1976.

_________, *Report of the Review Committee on Regional Rural Banks*, Bombay, 1978, (Chairman: M.L. Dantwala).

_________, *Report of the Study Team on Agricultural Credit Institutions in Orissa*, Bombay, 1981, (Chairman: M.V. Hate).

R.B.I., *Statistical Tables Relating to Banks in India*, 1975 to 1989.

(iv) Other Bank Publications

Puri Gramya Bank, Pipili, Puri, *Annual Reports*, 1970 to 1990.

Index

❑❑❑